"Ms. Senter's debut offering is a tour-de-force of color, emotion, and longing. The generational impact experienced by the characters is tied together neatly starting with the cantankerous, aged, mom, Sophia, who we see at the beginning and all the way to Honey's freedom plunge at the end that illuminates her soul and frees her heart. It's an entertaining and very worthwhile journey of discovery with themes of survival, redemption, and lessons of the higher self that will have you enthralled. The southern world of Sophia, her parents, and her progeny is captured vividly and realistically like magnolias in the springtime. A buffet for the senses, folks who grew up in the South at this time (particularly in the Savannah area) will recognize the images and be transported back to their childhood. For all those who yearn for closure, acceptance of self and others, as well as a sense of peace, and calm, just take a walk down *Salt Creek Road*. The marshes will sing to you. Theirs is a song of empathy, compassion, and discovery."

–Steffan Richmond Oxenrider,
Author of *Dead Reckoning*

When you meet Honey Jo, first you can't help thinking, *Man, she is a tall beautiful woman.*

What you really remember is her kindness, warmth, and wisdom, and of course her childlike laugh.

Everybody has a story, and I've heard thousands. I got the book one evening and immediately started reading. I could not put it down. Hours later I was overwhelmed with feelings of love for Honey Jo, her mother, her father, and the rest of her family. They just did the best they knew. Honey Jo, thank-you for reminding me what love can do and having the knowing of something better. You have the ability to trust God and the process of the journey. You are very brave.

Karla Hillen, LCSW, Owner of Richmond Hill Family Counceling Center, Richmond Hill, Ga, and therapist with over 30 years experience on her own journey back to love.

This is a fascinating book that has a dramatic turn for the better at the end. As I was reading it, I began thinking. *My God, does this person and her family ever do anything right? Why does she continue to make the same mistakes over and over?*

I began to feel sorry for her, certain this story would not have a happy ending. And then, boom!

A fabulous ending tied together all of the dangling threads, as the author discovered how to negotiate her own "Salt Creek Road" to satisfaction, security, and sanity in a new world for her.

—Bill Worth is a writer/editor who has published three books on Amazon: House of the Sun: A Metaphysical Novel of Maui; The Hidden Life of Jesus Christ; A Memoir; and Outwitting Multiple Sclerosis: How I Healed My Brain By Changing My Mind.

Many people will be blessed and forever changed after reading this story.

—Best-selling author, Tom Bird and creator of
the Write a Book in a Weekend Retreat.

Salt Creek Road

HONEY JOSETTA SENTER

This book is dedicated
To my mother
And
All who seek freedom

Contents

Author's Note

The book you are about to read is based on a true story. The moments are reflections of mine, a collection of a lifetime of memories shared throughout my growing up years by my mother, and some of my own experiences as a child, adolescent, and adult. Each of them flashed before me as I was graced through forgiveness with a new appreciation for her and the life she's lived, some of it prior to my arrival.

Salt Creek Road embodies these recollections of mine, some of which have been compressed partly due to lack of knowledge or information about the persons or times, and another part to protect the privacy of those involved. The names have also been changed for this reason.

With a genuine intention to keep you entertained, I took the liberty of adding a bit of literary color here and there. However, the message conveyed remains the same. This is my hope for you who read this story.

It's never too late to change, miracles really do happen, and hope always prevails.

Enjoy your journey down *Salt Creek Road.*

Acknowledgments

It's with a heart full of gratitude that I wish to acknowledge the following for all of their assistance directly or indirectly that led to the realization of this book.

To God for giving me the lifelong desire and inspiration to write.

To Steffan and Libby Oxenrider for encouraging my sisters and me to get this story out there, and for the continuing encouragement and validation all along the way.

To Paula Tate for bringing the message of Tom Bird to our home, and for sharing her amazing experience of completing "How to Write a Book in a Weekend" with Tom at a writing retreat in Arizona.

To Tom Bird for the gift he promised to use: To help others find their way to the pages that lie there waiting. Tom has a unique way of leading us to the answers in our hearts.

To my sisters for supporting me and holding space for the dream of completion.

To my sweet friend Joyce Ann Leaf for softly kicking me in the butt when I doubted myself. She knew about and believed in this book before I did. Thank you friend.

To my children, life's most precious gifts to me. Thank you for the encouragement and tech help!

To my best friends Connie Gartman and Jill Morrow for your help and for listening.

To Anthony Register, thank you darling for giving me all of the space and time required to get it done.

To all of this life, the many homes, friends, relatives, jobs, schools, clubs, husbands, teachers, and beaches that made this story.

Thank you all.

Prologue

I set the alarm for five a.m. to "make time" to meditate before starting the day. Monday is the day designated to go to my home in Springfield, Georgia to see about the needs of my disabled mother who lives there. It seemed I'd just closed my eyes and the alarm clock was already sounding. I hit the snooze button and drifted off to sleep again only to have a quick dream. My boyfriend Tony and I were in a jewelry store. "Why are we here?" I asked him. "Choose something nice for yourself," he answered. I looked through all of the glass cases for something to grab me. I remember thinking *I wish he would just buy for me what he wants me to have.* The alarm clock went off again at that point. I fumbled around to find it on the bedside table and hit the off button, closing my eyes with hopes of just five more minutes of the dream. It didn't happen. I couldn't go back to it. Dang it!! What did it mean? *Was he going to propose to me?* My thoughts continued to dance around trying to figure it out. Dream interpretation has always been an interesting subject to me. It's like decoding the mysteries of the subconscious mind. I was going over the details of the dream again while putting on my robe and shuffling to the kitchen for a coveted cup of coffee. As Tony and I sat quietly in the living room sipping the meaning of the dream came to me like a gentle Ahhh-haaa moment. I have to choose something really nice for myself, something "I" have always wanted, a nice life, a happy life, a healthy life. It should be a playful life, full of laughter and enjoyment. It has to be a choice. No one else is going to choose it for me. It's going to be what I make it. I suppose I've always been okay riding on the shirt-tails of whatever someone else chose for me now that I think about it. It doesn't seem as though I've ever made my happiness and satisfaction with life my own responsibility. Wow! That's quite an epiphany for five o'clock on a Monday morning. *Who needs meditation after that?* I thought.

I shared the dream analogy theory with Tony. "I'm going to marry you one day darling," he said. He turned the TV on for his news fix. I just laughed to myself as I headed to the shower. He didn't even get it. *We are from Mars and Venus* I thought. I shook my head and smiled. My attention was shifting to the day ahead and remembering that I'd scheduled someone to come in for a massage at the chiropractor's office where I rent space. This client was the daughter of a couple who'd been clients of mine for quite a while. The mother told me her daughter remembered me from Savannah Christian private school. *Must be the name* I thought. *Not many people named Honey Jo, besides, I was only there for one school year.*

Laurie Chadwell showed up right on time for her appointment. She gave me a big southern hug as soon as she walked in saying "Oh my, Honey Jo! You really look the same." She was bubbly and friendly, so completely southern. I smiled back. I looked into her eyes, searching my memory. She looked somewhat familiar, but I wouldn't have recognized her on the street in passing. A few minutes after her massage started she began to share a memory with me from our second-grade school days. She said "You were a chunky girl like me, and we were at the swimming pool at school. You were wearing this bikini. It was blue with little red hearts on it. I wanted to be just like you because you were swimming, laughing, and having so much fun. I sat on the side of the pool with a T-shirt on, covering my suit, and my body. I wished I could have been more like you." I was so taken aback by the details of Laurie's second-grade memory that it left me speechless for a while. *That was more than forty years ago!*

I didn't remember the suit or swimming in the school pool. What I did remember was that somehow from that moment to my teenage years I too became the girl on the side of the pool covered with a big T-shirt. I thanked her for sharing the memory.

I'm now on my way up to Springfield to see mama. Springfield is a sleepy little country town about thirty miles north of Savannah. I call it Mayberry. The sidewalks roll up at dusk. Downtown is full of antique shops, a small hair salon, bakeries, and small cafes. There is even an old restored movie theater, a small two-pump gas station, and a Huddle House breakfast place where one can go to catch up on all the latest town gossip. For some reason I'm feeling a bit dreadful about going up there today. I'm feeling a little bit anxious. I decide to keep driving even though the idea of going back to the home I share with Tony feels like the best choice at the moment. After nearly twenty-three years of being a massage therapist and self-help publication junkie I've learned not to give in to those fearful thoughts and feelings but to go into them and see where they come from. So I reach into my imaginary alternative therapies toolbox. It's the place where I store all of the different techniques to handle an array of ailments. I can self treat everything from hangovers to depression with the tools I have in there. I pulled out some positive affirmations coupled with some deep belly Pranayama breaths, and a few huffs of Lavender essential oil in hopes of invoking the parasympathetic nervous system response of "relaxation" that I felt I needed so badly.

I pulled into the hidden driveway and there it was, tucked behind a wall of azaleas and surrounded by nearly a hundred evergreen camellia bushes. It was my sweet little house. I felt an instant connection with this little house when I bought it nearly fifteen years ago. It was a lovely place to heal after my last break-up. So simple and sweet. It gave me a nurturing welcome like grandma's house, like a grandma's hug. It just felt good, and I could afford it.

The little house had recently undergone a complete renovation. The last big hurricane that came through downed several big trees and damaged the roof. There was water damage on some of the interior walls of the house and the little outside office. Tony, my boyfriend ... I really hate to call him that. He is more than a boyfriend but not a husband. We've been together for ten years now. I must come up with a name for that in-between boyfriend and husband's place. Not a partner, or a friend, or a soul mate ... yes, he is all of those things, but I just don't like the worn-out, familiar verbiage. I'll come up with something. Anyway, he is a developer and building contractor, so he lent his subs and materials at his cost to me for the extensive re-do. That coupled with the insurance covered a new roof, so with a few commissions from my second career as a Realtor we were able to re-do the entire house. Me, my two daughters, their husbands, and my father did all of the demo work. We put it back together with handicap features to accommodate my disabled mother's needs. She was all but homeless at the time living on a small Social Security disability pension.

I park the car and go inside. All of the blinds are pulled tightly shut just as they always are. No lights are on in the main part of the house and my eyes try to adjust to the darkness. It smells stale and feels dungeon-like. She keeps herself closed up in the larger of the two bedrooms and the bathroom between them. Sometimes she's been closed up in there so long the Co2 detector will sound an alarm. When she calls me about it I tell her to open some doors and let the airflow throughout the house. I notice that the trash can beside her bed is full. There are things dropped around the bottom of the can on the floor that she couldn't pick up. The small fridge she keeps on top of the dryer in the bathroom has old food in it that needs to be disposed of. "Where is your help?" I asked her. She said, "that bitch started doing more and more things her own way! She wouldn't listen to a word I said. She came in here demanding I get up and take a shower. I told her I didn't want to take a damn shower right now! My head was hurting and then I told her I didn't need her services anymore. I thought I was getting a helper, not a damn drill sergeant! I'm never comfortable taking showers while she is here anyway. She takes pills, and I'm afraid she'll steal my pills while I'm in the shower."

"Mom," I said, "this happens about every two months. You love them when they start. Then within two months you are calling them every name in the book."

"I can't help it, they're ignorant," she said. "They don't know how to cook, they don't know how to shop. One girl didn't even know what pimento was for Christ's sake!"

I listened to her rant about the last aide she had, and the one before that. Then she started complaining about Buddy my friend who cuts the grass for me. We trade grass-cutting for massage therapy for him and his wife. "He lets grass cuttings fly into my pool out there," she said. *I knew you would never ever be able to get into the damn pool to begin with* I thought. *We put it in any way just to make you happy!*

If I had to choose an archetype for my mother, it would most definitely be the Queen from *Alice in Wonderland*. She is quite entitled to the best of everything. When it's not provided, OFF WITH YOUR HEAD!!

I could feel my energy seeping out slowly, like the air in a tire with a big nail in it. I cleaned up the mess and took out the trash. I quickly went to the store and bought some things for her to eat that she could manage without assistance until the company could find a replacement for the aide she fired. This sometimes took a while. She wouldn't have anyone back who had been there before, so they would have to hire someone new to assist her. I helped her take a shower and put clean linens on the bed. We talked about her little parakeets for a while and then I left to go back to Richmond Hill and Tony. I felt so completely drained when I left there but remembered yet another remedy from my trusty toolbox. Epsom-salt baths were something good to remove negative energy from your mind, body, and spirit.

I walked into his house and headed straight to the oversized tub in his bathroom to draw a bath. I flung two heaping cups of Epsom salts into the water and then headed to the kitchen where I poured myself a glass of red wine. *Why was I having such a hard time with this* I thought. I've been *A Course In Miracles* student for a long time now. I'd just finished the exercises in *Write to Heal* by Tom Bird. Intellectually I'd forgiven both of my parents. I know that people don't have children and then say, "let's see just how screwed up we can make them!" They do what they can with what they have, but often pass on the same belief patterns and behaviors their own parents had. I'm sure I did some of the same with my own children, at least until I learned how to change my beliefs. Now I'm beginning to see a correlation with the dream I had this morning, the memory Laurie shared with me during her massage, and what's happening right now with my mother. It's about choosing my own happy life. It's about not sitting on the sidelines covered in a big shirt giving my power away to what others might think of me. Spending time with my mother always made me want to start exercising and make better choices for myself so that I don't end up like her. What I was feeling now felt so much deeper than anything I knew with my intellect. Like a gemstone vein that runs deep in the earth, this was deep in my soul. I began to sweat profusely as I lay there in the hot, salty water. My voice began to give life to the buried feelings about her. Like a volcano of pure hate it began to spew out of me. I'm ANGRY!!!!

I didn't have a stable childhood!

I went to thirteen different schools before dropping out in the ninth grade! I was smart! I should've been successful and educated!

I got kicked out of Savannah Christian private school that my father was paying for because I was missing too much school. In the second grade!

I'm angry that you didn't make me go to school!

I'm angry I NEVER felt safe unless we were living with Granny and Papa.

I'm angry you lived in such violent relationships and I had to witness those awful fights! I was so afraid!

You didn't take care of yourself! Now I'm having to care for you because of it!

I'm angry you NEVER take responsibility for your life or health. It's always someone else's fault!

I'm angry you don't have relationships with your other children, and it's all up to me to care for you.

I've been your protector my whole life! I had to call 911 to protect you when I was just a child!!

I'm angry you sent me to live with other people while you sorted out your life!

I'm angry we had to live in efficiency motels!

I'm mad you never finished a book or a painting. You could've supported us with your talent.

I'm really angry that you asked me if I wanted to go live with my father and when I said "yes" you locked yourself in the bathroom of that motel room and cried and wailed. I felt my honesty and truth hurt you so badly. It was a horrible way to manipulate me!

I'm angry you never took my father back to court. Who cares if he threatened not to have a relationship with me like you always said? At least we wouldn't have moved so often because you couldn't afford good housing! Children don't make the rules. The parents do! Even if it's something the child won't understand. It's what's best for their welfare. We would have been better off. You gave up!! You always GIVE UP!!

There it was in its entirety. I just lay there open and vulnerable. A floating feeling came over me as tears began to stream down my face. All of that energy released was creating a shift. As the moment slowly passed I was able to view my mother's life with compassion and empathy for the first time ever. I knew deep inside that forgiveness was happening. There didn't seem to be anything I did to call it in other than feeling what I didn't even know was hiding so deep within me. It just landed there like a floating feather on my heart. Forgiveness.

Her life and the stories I heard her tell over and over throughout my life began to flash before me. I could see how history repeats itself, generation to generation. I was able to look without judgment into the moments that made her so cold, bitter, resentful, and full of revenge. I was able to see how holding on to all of the hurt and disappointment from her past was causing the hell that she's living in now. This is what I was shown.

Forgiveness frees us personally. It's through our own expectations of others that we become disappointed, hurt, and feel betrayed. The only way to escape these negative emotions is to "let go" of the perceived harm caused by the other which really came from our own expectations that the person should have behaved differently. That somehow we were entitled to something better.

As adults we must become "all right" with who we are through our own choices, self-discipline, and self-government. We need to learn that no one else is to blame for our own imprisonment and suffering. We must each choose the lives that make us feel peace and joy. We must do it for ourselves and for the generations that follow.

This story is based on a true story.

I was about fourteen years old when my mother decided to tell me about the child she had to give up for adoption and the reasons why. She called me into the kitchen and asked me to sit at the small wooden kitchen table with her. "I have something to tell you," she said. "I believe you're old enough to understand now."

CHAPTER 1

Jesup, Georgia

The year was 1965. My mother Sophia watched the calendar closely. She knew it had been exactly nine months to the day she'd conceived. She called her mother Doris to make the drive from Savannah to the small southern town of Jesup to pick up my older sister Marilyn who was eighteen months old at the time. Mom knew Doris would take good care of Marilyn, but saying goodbye wasn't easy. She and Marilyn hadn't been apart for more than a day since her birth. Mom loaded my sister along with her bags in her mother's car and told Marilyn to have lots of fun with Granny and Papa. Marilyn gave her a big hug around her hugely pregnant belly. My mother watched her mom's car until it disappeared in a cloud of dust on that dry, hot June summer day in Georgia. She watched until the car completely vanished and dried the tears from her eyes as she walked back inside the house.

The very next day late in the afternoon she began to have some lower back pain. Jane, the kind lady she was living with during the last few weeks of the pregnancy, quickly called for a sitter for her own children. She drove my mom to the hospital in Jesup. By the time they arrived her pain had really increased. She was having hard, steady contractions. She asked to please see her doctor. The nurses went out of the room to call but came back to explain he would be a while getting there. The OBGYN she'd been seeing during her stay in Jesup had promised her she would be put to sleep soon after her arrival. He promised she wouldn't remember anything. She wouldn't have to labor, she wouldn't hear any crying babies, and it would all be taken care of so that she would have little to no recall of the entire experience. Knowing that second babies often come faster than first ones and with the nurses now telling her it would be a while before the doctor arrived she began to freak out. She started screaming and was flailing about the room knocking things over as she shouted "He promised me!!! He promised me!!! No pain!! No crying babies! He lied to me!"

The nurses were all running around frantically trying to calm her down. They came in to put a mask with a drug in it over her mouth and nose. The drug in the mask didn't take any of the experience away for her. It only made her feel loopy and drunk. With a wild and crazed look in her eyes, she began talking to the child trying to emerge from her body, "I will always love you! I will never forget you!" Her teeth were chattering and her body was trembling. She was visibly distraught, crying, and bracing herself through each contraction. Then, lights out.

My mother awoke in a sterile-smelling hospital bed on the orthopedic floor. Still feeling kind of drunk from the anesthesia, she remembered a portly middle-aged nurse coming in and flipping through her chart. As she looked down her nose over the top of her glasses the nurse asked accusingly. "What kind of back surgery did you have?" She felt as though the nurse already knew the answer but was hoping to shame her. "You mean, old, crotchety thing!" mom said. "Get out of my room!" Slowly she reached down to feel her abdomen, sliding her hand back and forth, and then in large circles all around the circumference of her stomach. She longed to feel the life that once filled her. There was no way she could've ever been prepared for the emptiness she felt. Was it a boy or a girl? Was it being held or nurtured the way she would be holding and nurturing it? She felt so much pain for the loss, soo much regret. When the doctor came to make his rounds she told him about the accusatory nurse and her questioning. He assured her the nurse would not be coming back to her room, and she thanked him for that. The doctor decided to keep her for five days after delivery to monitor her mental state. She'd required sedation on several occasions, just like many of the other young ladies having adoption deliveries in Jesup, Georgia.

CHAPTER 2

The move to Savannah

It was 1945 when my mother's father, James, decided to move back to Savannah. The family had all been living a mighty fine life in Canton, Ohio. Her father moved to Canton after being offered a teaching position at an equestrian estate there thirteen years earlier. The well-known millionaire Mr. Groover spotted the young agile Papa of mine playing polo with some gentlemen in Augusta, Georgia. Mr. Groover liked the way Papa handled horses, as well as his genuine likable personality. Papa James had taken a leave from his boxing career. His doctor told him he'd over-trained and didn't have an ounce of fat on his body. He was burning muscle for fuel and was risking burnout. Considering the fact that his boxing career may very well have been over, he made a decision. He took Mr. Groover up on the offer which included room and board in a garage apartment and a generous salary.

His love of people and horses made him a natural teacher. He was a fun-loving guy who loved to play pranks on people he was close to. He told a good story and a good joke too, sometimes both at the same time. He was a nice-looking man, tall, distinguished, and well mannered in a southern kind of way. He was the epitome of Southern charm.

Once he got settled in at the Groover Estate in Canton, he began writing letters to the young lady named Doris whom he'd been courting back in Augusta. She was nine years younger than he, but age didn't seem to matter. She'd been completely captivated by James and his charming ways.

Doris went to work at the phone company in Augusta as a switchboard operator at the age of fourteen after her mother passed away unexpectedly. When she turned nineteen James asked for her hand in marriage. She was elated and accepted his proposal with delight. They married in Augusta and she joined him to live in the garage apartment at the equestrian estate in Canton. They lived there until they saved enough money to buy a piece of Ohio land with a house and a big barn on it. Papa James then opened his own riding academy. He and Doris hired work hands who lived in the bunkhouse down in the barn. The workers shoveled stalls, groomed, fed the horses, and helped keep the property proper, and pristine. The clientele were the wealthy ones who could afford those kinds of horses and the lessons that went along with them. Doris got pregnant right away. She bid farewell to her nineteen-inch waist as they welcomed their first child, a boy named Roger.

My mother often retold a funny story she heard her father James tell many times. Little Roger was about five years old. He wanted to go to the horse auction with his father and the workers, but Papa James told him no, he was not allowed to. Little Roger, mad about his father's decision, took his small child-sized pitchfork and flipped some soft manure onto his father. Realizing what a big mistake that was just as soon as he did it little Roger took off running. He took refuge in every nook and cranny where his oversized father James couldn't fit to get him! Finally Roger got brave enough and took a chance. He struck out running up to the main house with his daddy hot on his tail. Roger ran around and around the house. Every time he passed the front door of the house he hollered "Mama! Open the door! Mama, open the door!" His father got so tickled and started laughing so hard he couldn't chase him any longer. Doris stepped out on the porch to see what all of the commotion was about. She was wearing a big flowing skirt. Roger ran straight up the stairs, and right up the back of her skirt. He stood as still as he could clenching her legs. Papa found the whole situation way too humorous to even bother trying to spank him.

They had a second child by this time. She was two and her name was Peggy. Roger loved his baby sister. They would grow up together learning how to ride horseback and having all types of outdoor adventures on their farm, and the farms neighboring theirs. The riding academy business was lucrative. Papa taught English riding and jumping.

Doris was accumulating all kinds of fine furnishings, and beautiful dishes for the large two-story house. She was wearing the best clothing, and so were the children. They were both surprised with a third pregnancy and nine years after Peggy came they had another girl. This was my mother whom they named Sophia.

For reasons still unknown to anyone when my mom was just six months old her father came in from work one day and told her mother to pack the kids and what belongings she could fit into the vehicle. He'd sold everything, the house, the riding academy, their furnishings, all of it. They were moving to Savannah! They would be moving into a neighborhood where his brother Earnest and wife Margie lived. Silk Hope Farms was the place, so named by the early settlers of the area who had hopes of producing silk from the worms that would feed on the White Mulberry trees planted there. Silk Hope was not too far from downtown Savannah. It was a blue-collar neighborhood. The families there were hardworking, God-fearing, and close.

James and Doris were able to purchase a small home outright on Salt Creek Road with the proceeds from the Ohio sale. It was a small one-bedroom, one-bathroom, batten board home on a sizable 11-acre plot of land that backed up to a marsh and creek. There was also a small stick-built room that appeared to have been an old classroom at one time. It was complete with a small front porch and a blackboard inside. It would become known as the playhouse and sat just off the left side of the small house. Papa James promised Doris they would add on to the house as money allowed. The move would be a thorn in Doris's side for countless years to come. She would often bring up all that she'd given up in Ohio naming brands of furnishings, clothing, and the like. She couldn't believe that her fine Ohio life had been traded for what seemed like a tiny little shack on a dirt road in the middle of nowhere - with three children to raise.

People often said to meet my grandmother Doris on the street it would be easy to assume she was a millionaire. She never left the house without her hair made up, perfect make-up, pressed clothes, a scarf of some sort, and some chic sunglasses. As a hobby she looked up a new word in the dictionary daily and used it to increase her vocabulary. There in Silk Hope she barely had a pot to piss in as they say, but meeting her outside of that neighborhood no one would ever know that.

She took a job at the new Sears and Roebuck downtown, the first Savannah business to have an escalator.

Papa James took a job delivering furniture for his half-brother Eric Brown who owned a furniture store on Broughton Street in downtown Savannah. The post-war economy was booming, and the furniture store was having record sales. This was enough to keep him very busy with deliveries and payment collections for things sold on credit. His charismatic demeanor made selling furniture and collecting the money for it seem effortless. Somehow they made it all work and were able to eventually add another small room onto the back of the house, but it didn't have heat and air-conditioning. The two girls would share that room, and their brother Roger slept on the couch in the living room.

Mom adored her brother Roger, but she was only five years old when he lied about his age and left the tiny home in Silk Hope to join the Navy. He spent several years on the USS Frybarger, of the United States Navy. It was a Buckley-class destroyer escort. Then after four years served he left the service to come home and marry his hometown sweetheart Judith. They started their own family there in Silk Hope also. My mother and her sister Peggy never really got along. Mom said she admired her sister Peggy's beauty and the stylish clothing she wore, but Peggy would often say mean things to her. She told her things like their mother never really wanted another child (meaning her). That she was a mistake. She said Peggy even told her once that their mother drank turpentine while she was pregnant with her trying to abort the pregnancy.

Aunt Peggy and mom both attended the Silk Hope Baptist Church. The only time my mother could ever remember her mother Doris stepping foot in a church of any kind was to see her and Peggy baptized. That church was also the place where Peggy met William Bartow. He was five years older than Peggy, but her father would allow him to take Peggy to the movies and to church functions as long as they let my mom Sophia tag along. Mom said William would offer her a quarter to cover her head at the movie. Once she came out of the cover just in time to see them stealing a kiss. William asked their father if he could give Peggy an engagement ring before he left for the Army. Her daddy refused, saying Peggy was too young. So, she and William said their goodbyes and promised to write to one another until he returned.

Peggy started behaving in a rebellious fashion after her father's decision to forbid her engagement to William. She snuck out of the house one night and walked all the way to a hotel room of a Navy man she and Doris had picked up hitchhiking down Hwy 17 which was the main thoroughfare to Florida. Mom said she was sure her mother must've been thinking of her own Navy boy and hoping someone would pick him up if he was in another town and needed a ride. Granny Doris knew that her daughter Peggy and the young man sitting together in the back seat were exchanging information to be pen pals while he was overseas, but she had no idea of the real plans being made. Peggy was only thirteen years old, although she didn't look thirteen. She was tall like her father and curvy like her mom. She didn't get caught sneaking out, but she did get caught when her period didn't show up! She was pregnant and the Navy man was long gone! Peggy wrote to him about the situation but got no reply. Mom witnessed how her father's heart seemed to be broken because of Peggy's unplanned pregnancy and her being so promiscuous at such a young age. To my mom, he seemed devastated. She vowed to herself she would never put him through anything like that!

My mother continued explaining to me how things were so very different back then. "It would be a disgrace to the family," she said. "Women were taught how to be a lady. How to look polished and poised. How to speak with proper English, run a sewing machine, cook good southern food, and never complain too much about anything in hopes of landing a husband that would secure a good future for them." There were even advice books and magazine articles like "Don't be afraid to marry young," "Cooking to me is poetry," and "Femininity begins at home." They all supported the collective mindset of the times. Education for women wasn't thought to be of much importance during this era in the south either. The desegregation of schools was just being enforced by the civil rights movement that began with the 1954 Supreme Court decision Brown vs. Board of Education. It ruled that separate educational facilities for black children were inherently unequal. She remembered the families of her friends being afraid of what would happen with both races together in schools. Some were so unsure of the changes happening that they let their daughters quit going to school altogether.

"To be an honorable wife was enough for girls her age to dream about," my mother said as she continued to explain the era to me. *Father Knows Best, Leave It to Beaver,* and *I Love Lucy* were the television shows being watched by young women. They were just getting the first televisions in their homes. Mom was twelve years old in 1957 when they got their first television. The shows were all a huge influence and modeled an ideal life for young women everywhere.

Secrets were another big theme then, and every family had them. Heck, her own mother hadn't even told her anything about having a menstrual cycle. When she started her period at age eleven she sat on the commode crying, thinking she was bleeding to death. "If your family had any so-called 'dirty laundry' you'd better not air it," she said. Everyone had to appear perfect. Appearances were what gave ladies their value in society's eyes. So to save her family's reputation and a bit of her own, her sister Peggy would marry Henry Redman who was much older.

Henry had always had a bit of a crush on Peggy and jumped at the chance to marry her, pregnant or not. He worked as a welder, earning wages that were enough for them to afford a one-bedroom apartment just off Whitaker Street in downtown Savannah to begin their married life together. So at fourteen-years-old Peggy was married with a son. She named him Monroe.

My grandmother Doris had gotten accustomed to having Peggy around to watch over my mother when she needed some space or time to herself. Now that Peggy was off and married, and Roger had joined the Navy, there wasn't anyone else to watch my mother, Sophia. Granny Doris would occasionally send mom to Peggy's apartment downtown to spend time with her new family when she felt she needed a break. Especially if she and Papa James were feuding about him coming home with a buzz on Friday afternoons as he almost always did. Mom said she loved to go to Peggy's. The streets were paved, and Peggy's husband Henry would spend time with her, teaching her how to roller skate and ride her bike. She said she felt special and loved the attention she got from Henry. Her own father was often too tired to play with her like that after work; besides, the streets at home were sandy dirt. There was no way to roller skate there.

Peggy's home was a one-bedroom apartment and she'd always slept with her little sister back home, she thought nothing of putting her little sister Sophia in between her and Henry to sleep for the night. Mom recounted the story with a vivid memory. Monroe started crying, and Peggy got up to nurse him back to sleep. It was then that Henry rolled over close to her and ran his hand up her thigh to her panties where he began to stroke her back and forth. She said she froze in terror, her heart beating so fast it filled her ears with a quick drumbeat. She said she just lay there pretending to be asleep as best she could, and silently

13

thanked Jesus for saving her when Peggy came back to bed. The next day Peggy walked into the living room of the small apartment to find her there rubbing her own belly with a tender sweet look on her face.

"What are you doing, Sophia?" she asked.

"I'm gonna have a baby," Sophia said glowingly.

"What on earth are you talking about?" asked Peggy.

"I heard mama say the reason you got pregnant was that Henry touched you down there. Henry touched me down there too," Sophia said.

No sooner did those words leave her lips, than Peggy had mom packed up and ready to go! She quickly drove her home with the strictest of orders not to tell anyone else what she had just confided in her. Peggy assured her little sister that she was NOT pregnant. "It doesn't happen that way, Sophia!" she told her. "Daddy will kill Henry if you tell!" Peggy said. So, Sophia promised Peggy she would not tell. The secret was like having cancer inside for Peggy, though. She thought of it every time Henry wanted to touch her. When she couldn't contain it any longer, she called her close friend, Pat, to confide in her all that had taken place with her little sister and Henry Lee. What she didn't know was that Henry Lee was just around the corner listening to her tell Pat the whole story. As soon as he figured out she wasn't talking to her daddy, or to the authorities, he rounded the corner and pushed the hang-up button down with one hand while he snatched the receiver from her hand with the other. He hit her in the face and head until she fell unconscious.

Peggy awoke sometime later, still on the floor. She got up and peeked through the rooms of her apartment to find Monroe asleep in the crib, and all of Henry's belongings and clothes were gone. He was never seen or heard from again. Peggy had to get a divorce by publication in the newspaper and move back home with baby Monroe to Silk Hope with her parents.

Mom said she loved having Monroe there. It was like having her own live baby doll to play with. She loved learning to change diapers, feed him baby food, and how to push him around in his stroller. As a result, they became very close.

Life moved on this way for several years. Mom and Peggy both started attending Silk Hope church again. It would also be the place where Peggy would reconnect with her first love when he returned from the Army. Peggy was overjoyed the day she saw William walk back in those church doors. Her admiration of him was obvious, so much so, that mom said Peggy nearly fainted when their eyes met. Mom said she gladly took little Monroe from Peggy's arms so she could run to William. The embrace seemed to last forever, she recalled. He was shocked to come back home to find Peggy divorced with a young child, but he didn't care. He still loved her. They courted again for a while, he proposed to her again, but this time he didn't ask her father for permission.

Mom said William wasn't much to look at, but everyone loved him. Everyone except her daddy. William would never take a drink with him. He just wasn't the drinking kind. Her daddy James said he would never trust a man who wouldn't take a drink. "William never did," she said. "He was a kind and gentle soul. He could play the guitar and sing Hank Williams' songs better than anyone." He and Peggy married and lived in Savannah for a while. William worked at the Greyhound bus station and then tried his hand at selling life insurance. He and Peggy were wasting no time having a family. As the children continued to come, and the funds to raise them got less and less, William decided to re-enlist in the Army. He became a supply sergeant. It was then that they began to move around, military style. The first stop was Perry, Georgia, then on to Fort Benning, Georgia.

My mother, being the last child at home with two working parents, remembers a young life full of chores and responsibilities. Every day after school she had cleaning and cooking to do before she was allowed to go out to play in the neighborhood with her friends. Her mother Doris cherished a clean home she said. She just didn't like to clean it herself.

Mom went on to explain how her artistic talents were recognized by her teachers in school. They wanted her to try out for the plays at the little theater in Savannah, Little Abner, Daisy Mae, and Dogpatch USA. They also wanted her to design and create the backdrops for school plays. Without transportation or after-school pickup, she wasn't able to take part in many of the suggestions of the teachers. She would have really been in her element doing things like that, but her mother and father didn't see the value in any of that so-called "nonsense." On another occasion, she was nominated for Military Queen at school by one of her fellow classmates. She was so excited to come home and tell her parents the news. She was already looking through McCall's' pattern books for what would be the perfect dress to make when her mother and father got home. Her father told her she would not be parading herself around in front of those boys at school for any such title, and that was the end of it! She retorted that he must have been an awful young man himself to assume those terrible things about everybody else! Her father gave her "the look" that said, "You'd better watch your tongue young lady or I'll watch it for you!" Embarrassed by her father's assumptions, she turned down the nomination at school the next day by pretending to be humble. Silently she blamed her sister Peggy for the way her father was treating her. *If she hadn't gone off and gotten herself pregnant at thirteen years old, maybe her father wouldn't be so strict on her* she thought. Strict was really an understatement. He had taken the telephone completely out of the house after Peggy's predicament. Anyone wanting to talk to my mother would have to come by in person, to the house. Her father would position himself perfectly, cleaning his shotgun within eyeshot of any boys that dare come "sniffing around," as he called it. It was as if he were talking about some ole hound dog rather than a human being, my mother recalled. The neighborhood boys were far too scared of Mr. James Wilson to ever ask her out. The few times she brought up the idea of a double date with one of her girlfriends, her father quickly shot it down completely.

People say that to have seen my mother back then it would be easy to understand why her father behaved in such a manner. She'd grown to a towering 5-feet-11inches tall. She had long beautiful blonde hair, and legs so long they earned her the nickname "high pockets." Her friends would often say she resembled the famous actress Brigitte Bardot, only mom was prettier. She had inherited her father's knack for jokes and storytelling, and her mother's beauty and style. As pretty as she was, she was also very much a tomboy. Her father taught her how to box, and she wasn't afraid to take on anyone who dared challenge her. Countless stories have been told of her rolling up her sleeves with the kids in the neighborhood if they didn't do things her way. "Fighting was their way to settle things back then," she would say. Parents thought nothing of it either. It was the kids' way of establishing a pecking order, just like animals do in nature. Speaking of nature, she also learned how to shoot a gun and hunt. She learned to fish, and she played ball with the neighborhood kids on the sandy dirt road in front of their home. They would all take refuge from the sweltering summer heat swimming in the tea-colored brackish creeks that lay just beyond the marshes of her backyard.

My mom and her mother Doris had a strange relationship. Mom always said she felt as if her mother was jealous of the relationship she had with her father. She said her mother did things intentionally to hurt her. For example, she would tell her that when she finished the chores on the list they would go somewhere and do something. Mom would eagerly finish the chores on the list, then her mother would add more things to the list rather than fulfill her promise. She said that mostly what she learned from her mother was that she couldn't be trusted. On other occasions, she said Doris would wait for her father to come home drinking and tell him about something bad Sophia had done. "It was like siccing an attack dog on an intruder," she would confide. He would get so frustrated, and then take those frustrations out by giving her a whipping with that leather belt that flew from his belt loops faster than a copperhead's strike, with a bite that was every bit as bad! When he was sober he never hit Sophia. He would have discussions about why the behavior was wrong and tell her if she repeated the wrongdoing again it would result in a whipping. She went on insisting that her mother Doris knew exactly how to push his buttons. Another time she recalled her father came home drinking and kicked her dog. Her mother cried out for her to come to the dog's rescue. "Of course I stood up to him," mom said. Her father then knocked her to the ground. She said she stood back up and stared deep into his eyes, the most deep, cold, stare. He knocked her down again, and again she stood back up and stared him down without a tear being shed. It happened over and over until her nose began to bleed and her mother begged him to stop hitting her. That was the last time her father ever touched her she said. She never blamed her father for what took place that day though. She blamed her mother for it all, calling her an instigator. Her father remained on a pedestal, as the good guy who was tormented by a nagging wife.

CHAPTER 3
"*1962*"
17 years old

Granny and Papa had been arguing again, this time to an extreme mom said she hadn't noted before. They were even talking about divorce! Knowing how sensitive she was to their quarreling, her mother decided to send her to Peggy's house at Fort Benning for a visit while she and James settled their affairs.

Mom caught the next Greyhound bound for Peggy's. She was filled with excitement to see her nieces and nephews. Especially that sweet Monroe she had been so blessed to bond with over the first few years of his life. Peggy also announced that William would be coming home from being deployed. Sophia was over the moon excited about that! She hadn't seen him in several years. Sophia welcomed the break from the constant turmoil with her mother and father back home. Sometimes she would actually dread the evenings there. Her mother bickering and her father coming in half-crocked and mean. Still, she blamed her father's drinking on her mother's nagging. "It was the only way he could tolerate her," mom would say.

Peggy met her at the Greyhound station with open arms and all four children in tow, Monroe joyfully calling her Nana ... Nana! Nana was the name he gave her as a toddler, unable to say "aunt." He leaped into her arms and wrapped around her like a little monkey. Then there was Peter, Sarah, and David for her to get to know as well. They laughed, shared stories of the recent goings-on, and played road games with the kids all the way home to Peggy's house. Mom always loved being with the children. She got to be a child right along with them. They made sand art pictures out in the yard, finding different colors of sand, dirt, and clay from the earth to create beautiful pictures. The butterfly was Monroe's favorite. They made things with finger-painting and baked peanut-butter cookies. Nana was a lot of fun to have around.

Peggy asked mom if she would mind sitting with the children for a few nights so she could go out with friends and enjoy some "adult" company for a change. Mom said she agreed with delight. As far as she was concerned there was never too much time spent with the kids.

She was sitting on the living room couch that evening just enjoying the silence in the darkened room. She was reflecting on all of the fun things she and the children had done that day when she saw headlights fill the room. Tiptoeing secretly over to the large picture window, she recognized the truck in the driveway as belonging to Mr. Ellis. He owned the service station on the corner. She quickly moved from the window and hurried to bed. She pretended to be asleep when Peggy peeked in to make sure all was safe and sound. Mom said she heard her mumbling something to herself but couldn't make out what she was saying. She heard her bump into the sofa table and knock a few of the photos over. *She must be lit!* she thought as she lay there wondering why her sister was spending time with that man. All my mother could see was how good Peggy had it. A loyal, providing husband who worshiped her. All of these beautiful children. *"Why is she doing that?"* she thought as she drifted off to sleep with all of Peggy's kids snuggled up around her like a mama cat with a litter of kittens.

The next morning she and the kids woke to the comforting smell of coffee and frying bacon. Peggy was cooking breakfast for everyone while cleaning anxiously between pancake flips. She was preparing for William's return. They enjoyed breakfast together, each of the kids showing her the artful creations they made with Nana as a surprise for daddy when he got home. Mom said she couldn't stop looking at Peggy. It was as if she were trying to bury herself in that hard head of her sister's to figure her out. Peggy must have felt her intrusion because all of a sudden she began to bark orders about how things would be when William got home. "Don't volunteer any information about my going out with friends!" She went on and on ... don't tell him this or that. Mom said the more Peggy ranted, the less comfortable she became. She loved William, and it felt like her sister was asking her to be deceitful. She couldn't do it. She wouldn't do it. So she waited for Peggy to go in for a nap to finish sleeping off the night before. She instructed each of the children not to go outside while their mommy was sleeping. She kissed them all good-bye and left on foot, suitcase in hand. She walked straight to the corner store and told Mr. Ellis she and her sister had a falling-out. She needed to borrow money for the bus fare back to Savannah. "My parents will refund you after I'm back home. I promise," she told him. Mr. Ellis pulled $10.00 from his wallet and told her he didn't need to be repaid. He instructed one of his workers to please come and give Ms. Sophia a ride to the Greyhound bus station. She felt she knew why he was being so kind and generous. He smelled of guilt and humility!

She boarded the Greyhound and made her way back about three quarters the length of the bus and sat down. She slid over to the window and made herself comfortable. There was a man sitting in the back of the bus who noticed her the moment she boarded. There was an obvious sadness about her, made even more obvious as the bus passed by the front of her sister Peggy's house where the children were all playing in the front yard. Silent tears streamed down her face as she watched the children from the bus window for as long as she could. Then, she heard his voice. "Excuse me, I see this seat is empty. Do you mind if I sit here?" he asked. She really was in no mood for company but remembering her upbringing, she could not be rude. "No, it's fine," she said softly. She moved her purse from the seat to make room for him. "I can't help but notice you're upset. Would you like to talk?" said the professional-looking man. "No," she said, "not really." Pausing for several seconds she added, "those children we passed back there are my nieces and nephews. I'm going to miss them, that's all." "Oh, I see," he said. He was thrilled that she was even considering a conversation with him. From the moment she stepped on that bus he wasn't able to take his eyes off her. *The most beautiful creature God has ever made* was all he could say to himself. *She had the body of a goddess, with skin, hair, and what seemed a personality to match. He had to find out more about her.*

"My name is Charles," he said. He extended his hand. "Charles McElveen."

"Hello, Charles," she said softly.

She extended her hand slowly and gently, introducing herself. "I'm Sophia Wilson." *This man is treating me like an adult,* was all she could think. That was something she hadn't experienced in her seventeen years of life. Just like her sister Peggy, Sophia's height and the way she carried herself made people think she was much older than she actually was. Charles interrupted her thoughts with questions about where she was from, her family, and her friends. She asked him why he was traveling to Savannah. He told her he worked at WSAW television station as an advertising executive. He went on to tell her he had graduated from Georgia Military School and had attended college at the University of Georgia. *What a really successful man,* she thought. She was impressed with the importance of Mr. Charles McElveen! He was ten years older than she was, but she didn't care. He made her feel special, important, and mature. They continued getting to know one another all the way to Savannah.

When the bus arrived Charles asked her if he could give her a ride home from the station. She agreed to accept his offer. Rather than letting him take her to her own home not knowing the condition her father might be in, she had him take her to a girlfriend's house just up the street from hers. Charles asked if she would accompany him to dinner for his birthday in a few weeks on June 14. She gave him her girlfriend Melissa's phone number to leave messages for her and told him that she would ask her father. If he would please leave a return phone number with Melissa she would call to give him an answer about the potential date. He waved goodbye to her as she stood there with her suitcase.

"Who was THAT?!" her friend Melissa said, barreling out the front door. "He was handsome! What a nice car! Do you like him? Because if you don't ... I DO!" her friend said with a big smile and a schoolgirl giggle. "Oh, stop it, Melissa," she said. She explained that he was just a nice man she met on the bus. She asked Melissa to take her home. She also asked her if it would be okay to tell her folks that she was the one who brought her home from the bus station too. Melissa just smiled at her knowing how strict her daddy was. She agreed to the request and completely understood.

Mom came home to a lecture from her mother. "Why didn't you tell your sister you were leaving?! Do you know how dangerous it is for a young lady to travel alone when nobody knows?" Her mother quickly noted a change in her daughter's demeanor. She seemed more self-confident, more mature. "Sophia," she said. "Have you met someone?"

"Why yes, mother," she said, "as a matter of fact I have. A very nice professional man who works for the television station here. He wants to take me to dinner in a few weeks to celebrate his birthday."

"Well!" said her mother. She had a big smile on her face. "Your father will need to meet him first. You should invite him to our home for dinner."

"Yes ma'am," she said. She looked down toward the ground, feeling small once again.

A few days later, Charles left a message for her with Melissa. She had been anxiously excited to hear from him, asking Melissa every day, "Any word yet?" She was craving the way he made her feel, like an important grown-up whose opinion and feelings mattered. Her voice softened in a naive way as she announced when she returned his call that her father would need to meet him before he would agree to any kind of date. Charles laughed and gladly accepted the invitation. He was no stranger to meeting new people. He knew how to make first impressions. Closing the deal after all was his job! Charles entertained everyone with tales of landing different advertising accounts for the station. He was quite a charming southern gentleman. The meeting went beautifully, and her father agreed to let her go to dinner with him for his birthday. It would be her first date ever.

That next Friday evening my mother and her parents all went to her uncle Ernest and Aunt Margie's house to have dinner. Stories of mom's new friend Mr. McElveen filled the air at the dinner table. They went on and on recounting all of his educational achievements and work history. They were gleaming with pride for their daughter's chance meeting. Mom said she felt as if she were literally glowing, and she wondered *is this what love feels like?*

Mom and Mr. McElveen went to the Johnny Harris restaurant on Victory Drive for the date celebrating his birthday. It was one of Savannah's most well known spots with booths surrounding a large circular dance floor. They always had a live band. It was the best place in Savannah for dinner and dancing. Anybody who was in the "in crowd" could be found there. She said they had the best date ever! It was the first date she'd ever had, but she was sure no other could have ever topped it. She felt like she was in heaven, and Charles was acting like he was too. Why wouldn't he? He had the most beautiful girl in the world on his arm. All of the turning heads in the room were proving that to him.

CHAPTER 4

Rumor Has It

Back in the neighborhood at Silk Hope, mom's Aunt Margie was talking with her sister Liz on the phone about mom's new beau. "That is an incredible coincidence," Liz said.

"What's that?" said Aunt Margie. "I am best friends with a lady here in Columbus at the phone company whose son is an ad executive in Savannah ... The only thing is, that man was just divorced and has a two-year-old son!" "WHAT?!" said Margie, "I've got to call Doris!" So, she did, and Granny Doris wasted no time sharing the news with mom's father, James. "I want her checked Doris!" he said. "However, you need to do that. Just make it happen!" he demanded.

The next morning while mom and her mother were in the small kitchen preparing breakfast together, she decided to confide to her mom. "I must tell you something, mother," she said. She wore a sheepish grin from ear to ear. "Charles and I had such a marvelous time at Johnny Harris, he told me he intends to marry me! He wants to ask daddy for my hand in marriage! Can you believe it, mama?" Her facial expression revealed her ever growing excitement.

This was the opportunity her mother had been waiting for. She told Sophia that before a woman gets married, it is imperative she have a complete examination and health screen. "I've heard there is a new lady doctor in town, the first lady doctor, in fact. You won't be ashamed about undressing if we schedule your physical appointment with her. I'll schedule it for you," her mother said. Mom just went along, believing what her mother was saying with such a matter-of-fact conviction. She said she was feeling more her mother's equal rather than her obedient child. She felt more grown-up and was really enjoying the independence of becoming a woman!

Her mother went with her to the doctor's office, and they were shown into the examination room. Once there, mom said she was instructed to remove all of her clothing. The nurse said to put this gown on the opening in the front, and lie on the exam table with the sheet covering her lower half. Her mother sat quietly in the corner of the exam room. The doctor came in and introduced herself, then gave mom instructions on how to place her feet in the cold metal stirrups on either side of the table. Further instructions came to scoot down to the end of the exam table until her bottom was on the edge. She said it felt awkward like she was squatting while lying down. The sheet made a tent so that she couldn't see the doctor's face, *which was a good thing*, she thought. She could feel the blood begin to rush to fill the cheeks of her face and neck. She was feeling absolute humiliation. The next thing she felt was the doctor trying to put something cold inside of her.

"What are you doing?!" she asked the doctor.

"I'm looking for your maidenhead."

"What is a maidenhead?!" Sophia hollered.

"It determines whether or not you are still a virgin," the doctor said.

Sophia became furious lying on that table and began to shout at the doctor. She was cursing like a sailor! She ordered the doctor away and laid into her mother with verbal fury as she pushed her body back onto the exam table using the force of her feet in the stirrups.

"How could you trick me like this? I can't believe you did that!! Goddammit, mother! You're something else! You can just go to hell!! Get me out of here!" she shouted. She all but leaped from the exam table putting her clothes back on as fast as she could. Her mother began to cry. "Your father made me do it," she said. "We've learned that Charles has been married before. He just got a divorce and has a two-year-old son! Your father wanted to be sure he hadn't taken advantage of you in any way honey. It was your father, not me."

That evening when her father came in from work Doris told him that his daughter was most certainly still a virgin, and that she was also extremely pissed off. He said he didn't care how mad she was. He knew what he needed to know. He went into the bedroom to talk to her, and he forbade her from ever seeing Charles McElveen again. She didn't say a word to him, only looked at him with that deep, cold, mean stare that seemed to say it all.

My mother was a rebel by nature. Her father's insistence on her never seeing Charles again was met with great resistance. The next day while it was just she and her mother in the house, she told her, "I'm going to marry Charles McElveen, and YOU are going to sign for me to do it!" It was as if this is what she expected her mother to do to make up for that doctor's office experience. Her mother didn't say a word, just stared back at her.

She and Charles scheduled a time to be wed the following month at the Chatham County courthouse. Granny Doris did show up to sign the documents giving her permission to marry him. She thought Charles was a good catch despite his former marriage and her husband's disapproval. She made the decision to deal with the wrath of James later and stayed to witness the courthouse ceremony.

The two of them lived in Savannah for a while, until Charles got fired. She said he swore up and down it was because he accidentally rode up and caught his boss with his secretary in the back of a car during lunch hour. Shortly after that Charles was given the pink slip.

It didn't take long for him to secure another job as an ad executive for Crock City Box Company, but that would mean they had to move back to his hometown in Columbus, Georgia. Charles decided they would live with his mother until he saved enough money for them to set up a house of their own. My mother wasn't happy with the idea of moving away from Savannah. She had never lived anywhere else, except for the time she was too young to remember during the first six months of her life in Ohio. She didn't like the idea of not being able to just drop by and visit friends or family but didn't put up too much of a fuss about it. She knew they had to go where the job and money were for Charles.

Charles's mother and Sophia mixed like chitlins and caviar. My mother saw her new mother-in-law, Donna McElveen, as fixed, superior, nasty, snobby, entitled, and very bitchy! Donna viewed my mother as a beautiful young child with no education, trying to get out of her poverty-stricken life by latching on to her one and only son! When my mother announced she was pregnant Donna got so upset she broke every dinner plate in the cabinet. Mom watched as they all crashed to the floor, thinking to herself *Damn, that woman is crazy!* She'd never witnessed such behavior. Later she was told that throwing things and breaking them was completely acceptable behavior for an angry, upset, southern woman. She knew it wouldn't have been acceptable in her house. Not with her father.

Charles's mom also took the liberty of buying everything they would need for the new baby. "It was always fine around that house as long as Donna was in control and making all of the decisions," mom said later. "She always seemed to know what was best for everyone. Especially for her son, Charles."

Mom delivered my sister, Marilyn McElveen, on June 22, 1963. She was so beautiful. Blonde hair, so blonde it was nearly white. Marilyn had beautiful green eyes. She was named after her father's favorite actress. It didn't take my mom long at all to fall in love with motherhood. She was having an easy time with breastfeeding and was wasting no time getting her girlish figure back.

Charles's grandparents on his father's side, Pete and Anna, came to meet the new baby girl. After witnessing firsthand how domineering Donna was with her new daughter-in-law, they offered Charles and my mother their vacation lake house that was located just up the road a bit to be used for their new family until they were able to get completely on their feet. Mom was ecstatic. She loved being near the water, and the idea of having her very own space to share with Charles and little Marilyn, well, yes, that would be great! Donna was furious when Pete told her of the offer he had made to them. *Thank God this will be the last fit she throws that I will have to witness,* was all my mom could think.

She and Charles moved into the already furnished vacation home. She really wished they had a phone but was so elated to be out of her mother-in-law's house that she wouldn't dare complain about a thing. Charles didn't share the same excitement she did. It was easier on him financially, and responsibility- wise to be at his mother's house. There weren't any living expenses. His mother did all of the shopping and cooking. She also made sure my mom and Marilyn had everything they needed. Charles's job required a lot of travel all around the southern United States. There were times when he would be gone from four days to a week.

There at the lake house, he had been gone four days so far this time. The groceries were running out, and mom said her breastmilk seemed to be drying up. She hadn't quite learned how to shop for planned meals and was on a tight budget to boot. She knew how to cook. Cooking was one of her chores at home growing up, but her mother always did the shopping and knew how much of everything to buy. Without a phone she just had to wait and hope he would come home. Several more days passed with no word from him.

She and Marilyn walked out onto the porch of the lake house and noticed a young girl across the way at the neighboring goat farm. They walked over to the fence to say hello. She greeted the young lady and asked what she was up to.

"Just milking goats," the girl said. "There's quite a market for it. Some folks get sick drinking cow's milk, but they can handle this just fine. Have you ever tried goat's milk?"

"No, I haven't," mom said. With a big smile, the young lady handed over a full Mason jar and told her to enjoy it.

"Thank you," she said, nodding in appreciation as she raised the jar to her as you might while making a toast. "I'll put it in the fridge right now," she said. She walked back to the house with Marilyn in one arm and the jar of milk in the other. As soon as she made it inside and closed the door she turned the jar up and drank every last drop.

The next day a lady named Sue she'd made friends with while they were living with her mother-in-law showed up for a spontaneous visit. Mom said she was so happy to see someone, anyone! She told Sue how her breast milk seemed to be drying up, and how she hadn't planned appropriately on her last trip to the grocery store. Sue was outraged to see that they were stuck there with no food, no car, and no phone.

"I don't know how to tell you this, Sophia," she said to my mother. "Charles is not working out of town. He has been at the softball games every evening. I saw him there playing with my own eyes." Sophia said she just sat there and listened in disbelief that her husband was in town. He was not coming home at night, not checking on his family, or their needs. She was devastated, to say the least. A tad bit embarrassed too!

"C'mon," said Sue, in an uplifting tone. "I am taking you and this baby to the store for some food.

You can come to my house to use the phone." So they went along with her to get a few things from the store. When they got to Sue's house, mom asked to use the phone to call her father. Sue tried to casually bend an ear to listen to the conversation. "Please come get me, daddy, I want to come home," she said. Briefly, she gave her father the details. He said, "Don't you worry, gal. I'm on the way." He stopped by to pick up his daughter-in-law, Judith, and the two of them headed for Columbus.

Sue took mom and Marilyn back to the lake house to gather their things. She thanked Sue for being so honest with her and for all the help. Sue told her again how sorry she was for the way they were being treated by Charles. The two of them gave a hug goodbye, and they vowed to stay in touch with each other.

Sophia devoured the few groceries she'd purchased earlier that day while she waited for her father and sister- in- law to arrive. Time flew by as she stayed busy packing things up for their return home. She was angry and hurt by Charles's actions but excited about going home all at the same time. She felt so betrayed by Charles. She was sure she wouldn't return as Columbus hadn't shown her anything she couldn't live without.

Her daddy and Judith had no problems finding the house. He told her when they arrived how much he liked the house and the property. He was always fond of the water, just like Sophia was. "Not a bad place to live," her father said to her.

"Yes," she said. "Not bad if you have a car, food, a telephone, and an honest husband!"

He just shook his head. "Wonder if that boy will ever grow up?" he said.

"I don't know, but I'm not hanging around to find out!" she said.

"I tried to tell you, I could tell he didn't live up to his responsibilities," he continued.

"Oh daddy, please don't do that I-told-you-so thing," she said.

He just nodded in agreement to drop it. She left Charles a note, but she was sure the news of her calling home for a ride would reach him long before he ever made it home to find it. It simply read:

We had no food. I know you were not working out of town. Marilyn and I are in Savannah. Don't call me to come back. I won't.
She signed it Sophia.

The four of them had a nice ride back to Savannah. *Her daddy was smart to bring Judith*, she thought. It kept her mind occupied so she wouldn't be consumed with thoughts of the situation she just left in Columbus. She and Judith laughed a lot on the way home. They shared all of the latest gossip of the goings-on in Silk Hope, and mom shared some things about how life had been for her in Columbus. Including the story of the wicked witch dish breaking mother-in-law Donna she had to live with from the beginning. They dropped

Judith off at her home which was just a few miles from theirs. Mom gave her a big hug and thanked her for coming along.

"Give that brother of mine a big squeeze," she yelled out of the window as she and her father drove off.

"I'll be back to visit y'all!!" Judith said. Sophia smiled back, waving and nodding in acknowledgment that she heard her.

Silk Hope never looked or smelled better. Mom felt the peace that home brings beginning to fill her as they rounded the corner of the sandy drive. Her mother Doris had been looking out the window in anticipation of seeing her daughter and her beautiful new granddaughter Marilyn. She quickly moved to the outside porch when she saw the car pull in and made it to the car with open arms. "Safe at home, safe at home," she said over and over. She hugged her. She scooped little Marilyn into her arms from the carrier and left Papa James and mom to unload the rest of their belongings. Mom thanked her daddy for coming to their rescue while they made their way to the door. She told him how good it felt to be home.

Mom never got the phone call she expected from Charles. Some part of her thought, *Surely, he would be calling to make some sort of explanation, and beg her to come back, even though she told him not to in the note she left behind.* He never called. She got more calls than she wanted from her mother-in-law Donna. She only seemed to be concerned with what my mother may be trying to get from them in some way. It drove Sophia crazy, to the point she didn't want anything but to be left alone from that bully of a mother-in-law!

More than four months had passed and still not a word from Charles. She asked around about who the best attorney was to draw up divorce papers. Jacob Krasnoff was the man everyone was talking about. He was moving up fast in the "best attorney" category in downtown Savannah. She called to schedule an appointment with him.

Jacob was quite taken with her beauty. He offered to help her free of charge even though she refused his advances. He counseled Sophia in terms of long-term needs: Educational expenses and health insurance along with what the Georgia law deemed necessary for child support payments. She agreed to all of Jacob's suggestions. She assigned the papers and sent them to Charles at his mother's address in Columbus.

By this time they had been apart for so long mom decided it might be best for her to look for a job. Her best friend Ivy was working at Hogan's department store downtown. Ivy convinced her to come in and apply. "I'll talk to the manager myself," she said. Ivy told the manager how beautiful and well-mannered her friend was. She told him how she was sure Sophia would be a good fit at Hogan's department store in ladies' accessories. The day she came in for an interview he hired her on the spot. She was hired full time at $1.25 an hour. They were paid every other week, a paycheck of about $75.00. It really didn't seem like much to her. Especially since she was paying Mrs.

Wilkins $15.00 a week to babysit Marilyn while she worked. Her mother Doris worked also so she couldn't be depended on to babysit. Sophia was worried about too much influence from her mother's ways anyway. Mrs. Wilkins lived just down the street from them. She was a sweet lady, and mom had gone to school with both of her children.

Three more months passed with no word from Charles about the divorce papers. Then one day the phone rang, and it was him. *At last. He has finally come to his senses,* she thought. "Come up to Columbus so we can talk, Sophia," he said. "Okay, Charles," she said. "I can do that."

Charles called the bus station and prepaid for hers and Marilyn's tickets. Her father gave her money for a hotel with instructions. "Don't you sleep with him! That's the only reason he is calling you up there, Sophia!"

"Oh daddy!" she said. "Your mind is always in the gutter."

"Listen to what I'm tellin' ya, gal," he continued. "I'll save you some heartbreak."

She just reached around him and gave him a big hug rather than argue with him. She was certain that Charles was going to beg forgiveness and ask her to come back and live as his wife again with their daughter Marilyn.

They arrived safely in Columbus. Marilyn was ten months old now. Charles was amazed at how much she'd grown. He lifted her up over his head looking at her beautiful little face. He told mom how she'd changed so much since infancy. Mom said she was rather happy to see Charles. He always had a way of making her feel acknowledged, as if what she had to say actually mattered in some way.

This was a feeling she rarely had living at home with her parents. She was patiently waiting for him to ask her to come back home as he drove them to his new apartment. She walked in with a feeling of awe at how quickly he was able to accumulate such fine things. He had art on the walls. Fancy dishes in the kitchen. *He must be doing really well at Crock City box company,* she thought. Soon after they arrived there came a knock at the door. Charles answered the door, and mom overheard a young lady explaining that her car had run hot. She needed some water for the radiator and wondered if he could help. Mom was listening intently from the living room and said she thought, *wait a minute, this place can't even be seen from the highway.* She rushed to the door and pulled Charles back by his shoulder so she could square off with the young lady. "You don't have an overheated car. You can't even see this place from the highway! Who are you, and what do you want with MY husband?!" With that she said the young lady took off running as fast as a lightning bolt back through a thicket of woods toward the highway.

She turned to Charles. "Who was that?!" she asked.

"It's the daughter of my secretary," he said. "That's where all of these furnishings came from. My secretary Betty lives here with me."

Mom said she felt complete humiliation. She thought he was asking her to Columbus to reconcile. "Take me back to the bus station, Charles," she said in a defeated posture, her voice barely over a whisper. "I want to go home," she added softly.

Charles asked "Will you please stay and see the attorney so we can get some papers signed? I'll get a hotel room for you and Marilyn."

"Yes," she said in a humble voice. "By all means, let's get this over with."

"What kind of child support are you asking for?" the attorney asked. They were gathered at his office. "I don't want anything," she answered. Her tough, prideful side didn't want any help from this scoundrel. "The state will mandate you receive a certain amount," the attorney said. "That's fine, whatever that amount is will be fine," she continued. She could feel the blaze of fury burning in her gut. She wouldn't even make eye contact with Charles. The attorney drew up the documents right then and there and got the signatures from both of them. Just like that, it was over. Now they just had to wait for it to be filed and a court date set. Charles took her to a hotel near the bus station and pre-paid for their fare to send them both back to Savannah.

Her father tried to console her as best he could but let her know that "things like this happen." She knew she would never forgive Charles McElveen.

"It looks like Marilyn and I are going to have to live back here at home with you and mama for a while," she said. "I will return to school and get a trade. I'll make you proud of me, daddy. I promise," she said. She looked up to him. It always bothered her that he might start comparing her to her sister Peggy. She didn't want to cause her father any of the kind of shame and remorse that Peggy had. Her father couldn't resist her heartfelt plea to return to Silk Hope full time. He didn't welcome the gossip about his divorced daughter that would be circulating, but he thought it would be nice to have little Marilyn there to spoil. The house was always too quiet with just him and Doris there any way he would admit.

Mom was really disturbed by all that had taken place in Columbus. She felt she had been tricked by Charles into getting upset and rushing to sign papers that probably weren't in her highest and best interest. His mother Donna constantly badgered her about knowing somehow she was planning to take her son to the cleaners. She thought about how she'd been so naive to think he was going to beg for her to come back. She'd been so sure of it she'd quit her job at Hogan's department store.

Her mother and father suggested that before she searched for another job or got tied down with school that she and little Marilyn should take a trip to Texas to visit her sister Peggy for a while. Aunt Peggy's youngest daughter, Gail, was just a few weeks older than Marilyn. The babies would both be celebrating their first birthdays soon. They told her it would make both she and her sister happy to meet one another's children and share some time. Even though mom and her sister Peggy never really saw eye-to-eye on much of anything she jumped at the chance to get away.

CHAPTER 5

Big Texas

Mom and Marilyn took the bus and arrived in Texas with a big happy welcome from Peggy who seemed to be brimming with a mischievous energy that was all but screaming "Let's go have some fun and excitement!" She was glad her little sister was old enough to go out to the clubs and play with her now. The two of them laughed, recounting stories of all the funny things the children said and did. How their mom and dad were doing, or not doing, and so on. Peggy appeared to be living the life. Beautiful home with top-of-the-line decor. She had the latest hairstyle and fashions for the season too. She and William had five children now. The two of them joked that William only needed to call home and Peggy would get pregnant! Mom was really happy to see her sister doing so well.

"Let's go out tonight," Peggy said. Her eyebrows danced up and down. "There is a great band playing on the base! What do ya say? We can dance and laugh. I can't believe you are old enough to go out with me now, sister!!" Mom agreed to go out on the town with her as she laughed at her sister's antics. Peggy made a call right away and arranged for a sitter. They had so much fun together getting all gussied up for the night.

"Look out Texas, here we come!" announced Peggy. "The Wilson sisters are here!" Mom just giggled at her continued theatrics. She was secretly very interested to see what Texas nightlife was like. This was the first time she'd ever been this far away from Georgia. All she could imagine about Texas were ten-gallon hats, longhorn cows, big belt buckles, and tumbleweeds.

"Maybe you'll even meet someone there," Peggy said.

"Well that is definitely NOT what I'm here for!" mom replied. She was certain of the fact she would never trust another man, ever. They laughed.

They were having a fabulous time at the club. The band was playing some great dance music. The gentlemen there seemed to be catering to their every need. Mom couldn't remember the last time she had so much fun. In fact, she was certain she'd never had this much fun. She was spending most of her time at the club with one of William's close friends who lived there at Fort Hood on base. His name was Marcus. He was doting and handsome. He was over six feet tall with an athletic build. These were the kind of guys she was attracted to back in high school but never got to date thanks to her father. Marcus had played football in high school and at Wake Forest in North Carolina. He told her in some of their conversations between dance songs that he was looking forward to trying out for the Atlanta Falcons soon after he returned from his deployment to Paris, France. He had lots of friends who'd already made it, and they were encouraging him to give it a go. The small talk flowed easily between them. He was a great storyteller, just like she was, and she had a great appreciation for that.

Everything was going great until she glanced over and saw her sister Peggy behaving in a way she deemed inappropriate with one of the men with whom she'd been dancing. She tried to make light of her sister's behavior to Marcus saying "Well, it looks like it's time to get Ms. Peggy back to the home front." She excused herself and made her way across the room where Peggy was with the man. She walked over and leaned into her ear whispering "It's time for us to go." Peggy just ignored her. "C'mon, we need to go home and check on the children. I'm never away from Marilyn this long," she said with a little more urgency.

"I'm not going anywhere. I'm having too much fun to leave now!" Peggy said. She half-drunkenly hung on the young man's shoulder. Sophia and Peggy ended up in a huge fight and caused a scene in the lounge before the manager asked them to leave. Mom said she did manage to get Marcus's phone number before they left the parking lot. However, she was so humiliated by the whole dramatic scene that she doubted they would ever talk again.

She lectured Peggy all the way home. "I can't believe you have all of this in your life, and you're out there screwing around on William! He doesn't deserve that, Peggy!"

Peggy fired back, saying, "You don't know what it's like to be alone all the time, little sister! Cleaning up after five children, cooking, all of the school stuff, and there's no one here for me. Well life is just too damn short for that! I'm gonna have some fun. If you are going to judge me for that then you need to go back home to mama and daddy and figure your own shit out! Get gone as soon as you can!!"

Mom said she could feel things were about to get out of hand as she imagined a fist-fight with her sister. She remained quiet for the rest of the drive home rather than push it. After Peggy went to bed she called the number Marcus had given her.

"Hello, Marcus?" she asked. "Yes," he answered. "This is Sophia. Do I remember you saying you had to go to Hunter Army Airfield in Savannah tomorrow?"

"Yes, you remembered that right," he said.

"Well I must tell you, I'm so embarrassed by my sister's behavior at the lounge. I just don't get her sometimes. Anyway, my daughter Marilyn and I could really use a ride back to Savannah. Do you think that would be okay? She's a very well-behaved child. I don't have any money to offer you. It's really an awkward position to be in. I just really want to get back home."

Marcus was quiet on the other end of the line for a few moments, and then clearing his voice he said "Sure, I could use some company. It will probably make the trip go a whole lot faster. I'll pick you and your daughter up at eight o'clock in the morning." Marcus thought she was the most beautiful woman he'd ever seen. Of course he would give her a ride.

"Thank you so much," she said. "You have no idea how much this means to me." She gave him the address, and they said goodnight.

Marcus arrived right on time. She'd been up for hours getting herself and Marilyn ready. She was writing a goodbye note to her sister Peggy when all of a sudden Peggy woke up on the couch, still half-crocked. She pulled herself up on the couch with smeared makeup and wild hair begging, "C'mon sister, don't be a baby! We were just having so much fun, don't go anywhere."

"No!" mom said. "You've said some very hurtful things to me. I'm leaving as you told me to so you can get back to your FUN life!"

Peggy reached out for a disappointing hug goodbye but mom just turned for Marilyn's stroller and walked out the door.

After getting Marilyn all settled in the back seat with books, toys, and snacks, she jumped in the front with Marcus telling him again how grateful she was for the bailout. They drove for hours, talking, playing music, singing along. They told each other jokes and stories, several really funny ones about William. She just adored William. He was everything a man and father should be in her eyes. Marcus convinced her to stop after several hours on the road to grab a bite to eat. He was happy to pick up the tab and was really enjoying her company. She shared her disheartening story about Marilyn's father and the impending divorce. He felt for her and the situation she was in.

An hour or so after being back on the road, the weather started to get nasty. It suddenly became really dark outside, and the rain was pelting the windshield so hard neither of them could see the road. Little Marilyn could feel their panic and began to cry. Marcus decided it was best to stop driving and get a room. They stopped in Selma, Alabama at the Days Inn. His own safety was one thing he thought, but now he had two other lives to look out for. It wasn't worth taking the chance. She insisted he only get one double room. Mom was feeling guilty about him paying for every-thing for them, and after all, they were only stopping to rest for a few hours to let the storm pass. She gave Marilyn a bath and put her down to sleep in one of the two queen-sized beds. She fell fast asleep in no time. Then mom said she took a shower and borrowed one of Marcus' big shirts to sleep in for a few hours. They only whispered softly to one another for a while as not to wake Marilyn, but she could tell Marcus was longing to touch her.

Her beauty and personality had cast its spell on him. She didn't resist his hands caressing her hair, face, and body. She relaxed into the memory of how it felt to be wanted by a man this way again. It had been well over a year since she had shared herself with Charles. They both gave in completely and fully enjoyed the open, vulnerable, passion-filled moments that followed.

When Marcus fell fast asleep Sophia quietly got up and moved to the bed with Marilyn. Lying there awake looking at the ceiling she was thinking, *This will be my secret. I owe him that much for all he's done for us. I can't believe that just happened!*

On and on her mind raced until Marcus woke up. The storm had blown over. He suggested they get a move on, and she didn't hesitate. Hurriedly she got Marilyn and their things together and made her way back to the car. The remainder of the ride to Savannah was unusually quiet except for the mental chatter in her mind that wouldn't stop until the wheels of his car made the turn into that sandy drive, and she was once again at home.

She was thanking Marcus for the ride home when her mother and father came out to greet them. Peggy had called ahead to tell them one of William's dear friends was giving Sophia and Marilyn a ride back home. Peggy told her mother she was sure Sophia was just homesick. Mom never told her parents anything different. They invited Marcus in for a bite to eat. He graciously accepted the offer. Afterward, they thanked him for returning their daughter and granddaughter and wished him well on his deployment to Paris.

Days and weeks passed, and mom was beginning to get some sense of self back, at least back to the place it was before she traveled to Columbus to meet with Charles. Her parents were enjoying happy little Marilyn as she learned to walk and play in the large, circular, sandy, dirt drive. Only an occasional call came from Charles's mother now. Mom couldn't wait for the divorce to be finalized so she didn't have to speak to that mean woman ever again.

Mom began to notice a little bit of nausea while her mother was frying bacon for several days in a row. She wondered if she may be getting sick. Sipping her coffee and picking at the hoecake and gravy on her plate, she wasn't really interested in eating at all. Then she glanced at the calendar her mother kept hanging by the back door. It was then she noticed her period should have come last week! It was as if all of the blood left her brain, she felt weak, pale, and clammy. She excused herself from the table and went to the bedroom to lie down. Her mother was puzzled about what had come over her and followed her to the room. "Sophia," she said, looking concerned, "What's wrong?"

"I can't talk about it right now Mama, please leave me alone," she said. Her mother hung her head and gently closed the door. She knew she would have another chance to talk to her when her husband left to go fishing with Leroy, his half-brother. Granny Doris didn't really like it when the two of them went fishing together because Papa James always came home half-drunk, and sometimes with no fish at all. She wondered if the two of them ever even made it to the water.

The time came for the guys to head out. Granny put Marilyn down for a nap. She quietly opened the bedroom door to find mom there writing a letter.

"Can we talk?" she asked.

"I don't know Mom, I'm so confused," she said. She was beginning to cry. "I don't know what to do. I made a mistake. I made a bad choice. Marilyn's father is going to take her away from me when he finds out. How did my life get so complicated Mama?" she asked through the tears.

"It'll be okay," her mother assured her. "You should tell me what's going on so I can help."

Sophia told her the entire story. Until now her mother believed she just got homesick, caught a ride home with a good samaritan and friend of William's. Now she learned her daughter is most likely pregnant. The father of this child has shipped off to Paris while she was still legally married to Charles. She was also being reminded that her oldest daughter Peggy was still wild as hell. Only now she is behaving that way in Texas, and not in the neighborhood of Silk Hope where the sought-after "good name" might be tarnished.

Granny Doris sat on the foot of the bed in disbelief, staring at Sophia with big eyes. When she finally did speak she said, "We'll talk more about this later. We'll figure something out. I won't tell your father a word of it. It would kill him. Don't tell anyone, Sophia. This must be kept our secret."

Doris left the room to schedule an appointment with a gynecologist to confirm her suspicion.

When the pregnancy was confirmed, mom began to cry on the exam table. The nurse tried to comfort her. "You know there is another way," the nurse whispered. "You don't have to have this child. You can have an abortion."

"No!" Sophia said. "I would never do that!"

Mom began spending most of her days in bed, trying to sleep away all of the circumstances of her life. She said she had many silent conversations with the child growing inside her. She was saying the same things to the child her mother always said to her: "I don't know what we're going to do, but we'll figure something out."

Granny Doris came home early one day after having met with attorney Jacob Krasnoff. "Sophia, you know attorneys are bound by law to keep your confidentiality. I really feel we can trust this man, so I told him in strictest confidence about your situation," she said.

"He said he'd already met you, that you had been in to draw up divorce papers with Charles, and that he also handles adoptions. He said he would be happy to help you, but he wants to meet with you first."

"ADOPTION?!" mom said.

"Well yes dear," said her mother. "Do you have any idea what it would do to your father to learn you are pregnant with a man's child whom you don't even know, while you're still legally married to Charles McElveen? Do you have any idea what people will say about you, about us? Your sister first, now this! There IS no other way, Sophia! You must!"

Sophia was furious with her mother. She slid on some shoes and headed fast out the front door with a loud slam of the spring-loaded screen door closing behind her. She took her shoes off and walked down the dirt road in front of her house. The road led to the creek where she and her friends shared so many summertime memories. The moss was blowing like long, curly hair hanging in the wind from the old oak trees. She began to pray and talk to God as she walked the warm sandy road in her bare feet. After all, she felt as though she had no one else to talk to. It was all a secret! She started praying.

"Dear God, please tell me what to do. Help me," she pleaded. Her heart was full of desperation. "I know I didn't do things the right way. The way you would have me do them, but I'm in an awful mess right now. I need your guidance, please ... please ... show me the way to make it all better. Let me know you are helping me with this baby growing inside me that I already love! Help me to keep this baby if there is any way I can. Tell me what's best for my child. Just tell me, please, please tell me."

By this time she'd reached the creek. It looked so abandoned to her. It was obvious to her no one had been there for a long, long time. She took off her clothes and left them on the now failing dock where she and her childhood friends jumped into the creek as kids. The sun felt glorious on her skin. The creek water seemed to cradle and comfort her as she stepped in, slowly walking in deeper and deeper. She took notice of the birds, butterflies, and the billowy clouds dotting the blue sky above. For the first time in months, she felt at peace. She swam for a while, engulfed in the serenity of the weightlessness from the warm, salty creek. She slowly swam to the edge of the bank and crawled up to lie on the old dock, letting the warm sun and soft wind dry her naked body. Only the sound of rustling leaves in the trees overhead, and the scurry of fiddler crabs on the marsh mud could be heard. She deeply breathed in the moisture-rich air and rested in the calm. Feeling transformed, she put her clothes back on, and slowly walked back home.

Granny Doris was in the kitchen and nearly cringed when she heard the door open, remembering the mood her daughter was in when she left the house earlier. "I'll go talk with Jacob Krasnoff, '' mom said to her mother. Her mother knew there had been a shift of some kind, but she didn't question it. She made the appointment with Jacob right away before mom had time to change her mind. He was able to schedule them that same week.

The two of them rode together downtown to Jacob's office. Mr. Krasnoff asked Doris to remain in the waiting room while he talked with Sophia in private. He asked her to recall every detail she could remember. The name of the soldier. What company was he in? Where was he stationed? What was his rank? Did he know about the pregnancy?

"I believe I may have a family for your child Sophia," he told her. "It may be another few weeks before I'm sure. They are a young Christian couple, unable to have children. They're quite well off. Not just good jobs but genuine family wealth. Your child would have a very comfortable life and never want for anything. Let's plan another appointment in a few weeks and we can settle the details at that time Sophia. The couple would also be paying for yours and Marilyn's room and board and all medical expenses in Jesup, Georgia. It's a little more than an hour away. You would need to plan to be there from the time you start showing until delivery. You would also need to watch your weight so you don't look entirely different when you return back home. Your mother has arranged for your father to believe you are in Augusta with your Aunt Eleanor."

She just sat there listening ... *Is this really happening?* she thought. "Okay, I'll see you then," she said. She walked back out to meet her mother in the waiting room.

Jacob didn't waste any time writing to Marcus Downs, the baby's father. He wrote to inform him of Sophia's condition. He told Marcus in the letter if he had any kind of honor and character at all he would return from Paris and marry her immediately.

Marcus was quite shocked when he received this letter from Mr. Krasnoff. He had his best friend pose as a priest and draft a letter of his own back to the attorney. The letter stated that he had only known Sophia for a brief time. He had no idea how promiscuous this woman was. He did not believe the child was his. He wanted nothing to do with the child or the woman.

This was the last bit of information Jacob needed before proceeding with the adoption. He needed to be sure the biological father would never try to interfere with the life of the child. He sent papers for Marcus to sign, giving up his rights to the child altogether. Jacob was ready to meet with Sophia again. He had his receptionist call to schedule another appointment.

Mom went to the appointment alone this time. Granny Doris stayed home to watch Marilyn. "Please," said Jacob. "Have a seat," he said. He gestured toward the leather chairs facing his desk.

He seems to be in an energetic mood, she thought, as she took a seat.

"I took the liberty of writing to Marcus," he said. "I wanted to see if he would consider coming home to marry you and give this child a name. He had his priest write a letter back to me stating that he was unsure of your promiscuity and he did not believe the child to be his. He has no intention of returning to Georgia for you or this child."

She had no idea Jacob was going to do anything of the kind. Her heart sank knowing Marcus had called her "promiscuous." She shrank thinking he thought she was anything at all like her sister Peggy.

She knew the truth though. She knew he had been the only man in her bed since Charles McElveen, and Charles had been the first. Remembering her long walk to the creek and her talk with God about the welfare of this baby she said to Jacob, "You say my child will never want for anything?"

"Yes, that's right," he said. "I realize this is a lot to take in," he continued. "If you need a few days to think about things I understand.."

She interrupted him. "Mr. Krasnoff, I think my options are running out. You said this was a Christian couple. My child will have the best of everything. I believe that is the answer to my prayer for this child," she said. Her voice cracked. "I'll agree to cooperate with you for what will be the best life for my baby."

"Okay Sophia, we'll need to give you a different name when you go to Jesup just so the father can never have a chance to make this couple's life a living hell," he said.

"I agree," she said. She was trying to hold firm and strong, but the tears rolling down her cheeks told Jacob this meeting had been more than enough for this beautiful young lady. He walked her to the door. She left his office feeling numb.

Questions filled her racing mind. *How could Marcus have thought she was promiscuous? She'd only known him for a day. How could he have known she wasn't trying to pin him down just to have an easier life for herself? Just like Donna her mother-in-law, always thought. How could she have been so naive when Jacob said he had written to him to think for a brief moment that Marcus may ride in on his white horse and save the day.*

The three weeks it took her divorce from Charles to be final felt like three years to her. *Time moves as slow as cane syrup when you are trying to hide a big secret from your father*, she thought to herself. It was a secret she was tired of hiding from everyone, so when she went to have her hair done with her stylist and dear friend Karen Metz, noticing they were the only two there, mom decided she needed a confidant. She trusted Karen, so she told her everything.

"Oh, Sophia," Karen said. "I'm so sorry this is happening to you. I can't imagine what you must be going through. I suppose the blessing is knowing that your child will be raised with wealth like that. It will have music lessons, the finest clothes, and schools. You know something else, Sophia." Karen said. "I have another friend who'll be living there soon. She's almost in the same boat. She's pregnant by a married man she was having an affair with. He's a businessman who lives just up the road in Richmond Hill. She'll be renting a house there in Jesup until the baby comes. I'm sure she could use the extra money your adopting family would be paying for your keep. Do you want me to call her?"

"Sure," Sophia said, "that would be great." Karen called her back a few days later with an address in Jesup. "Her name is Jackie Mullis," she said. "She would need weekly payments for your stay."

"Thank you Karen, you've been a great friend. I appreciate your help," Sophia said. Mom hung up the phone and called Jacob's office right away to give him the young lady's contact information. He would approve the living arrangements and make the financial agreements with Jackie for mom and Marilyn's room, board, and food.

At five months, mom was beginning to show almost to the point of not being able to hide it. It was time for the now Sophia Lucas and little Marilyn to make the trip to Jesup. Granny Doris would drive them there and return home, waiting for Sophia's call to make the hour-long trip back up to get Marilyn in time for the baby's delivery.

They arrived in Jesup in late February. The accommodations were better than she'd imagined. Jackie was a very attractive young lady, who was showing a good bit more than mom was. Jackie was a private lady who kept to herself most of the time. It was obvious to mom that she needed the extra money provided by their stay. It was also obvious she was in no way interested in trying to create a friendship. Mom said there was always a "business as usual" distance between them.

Time moved right along. Marilyn was one and a half years old now and into everything. She and mom spent a lot of time outside walking and going to the parks so they wouldn't bother Jackie.

One day as Jackie got closer to her due date, she came in to talk to Sophia. "You do know that I will be leaving as soon as my baby comes, right?" said Jackie.

"What!" mom said. "What am I supposed to do?"

"You'll need to figure that out," said Jackie. She turned and walked away. Mom immediately took Marilyn and walked across the street to talk to Jane. Jane was a very sweet young single mother who had befriended my mom the moment she and Marilyn moved in. Mom told Jane how Jackie was planning to take off after her baby came. Jane told her not to wait and worry about when that day would come, but for her to go over and get their things right then!

It would be fine for her and Marilyn to move in with her right away. Mom didn't waste any time. She returned and began packing. Jackie could hear the drawers opening and closing. The sounds of the clothes hangers sliding across the closet bar were enough to bring her back into the room.

"What on earth are you doing?" said Jackie.

"Marilyn and I are moving in with Jane across the street," mom said. "What about my weekly pay?" Jackie asked. "I guess you'll just have to figure that out," she said. Two weeks later Jackie went to the Jesup hospital to deliver. She never returned to the house.

Two weeks after that is when my mom knew it had been exactly nine months since the day she conceived. She called her mother to come up to get Marilyn. The very next day she went into labor.

It was time to go home from the hospital now. She gathered her few things, put them into the suitcase, and went outside to meet the car that Mr. Krasnoff sent for her. Driving the car was his protege, attorney James Louis Montgomery. In the back seat sat a young black lady wearing a nurse uniform. She smiled sweetly at my mom but remained quiet, holding yellow baby clothes in her lap. Mom thought *this must be the nanny for my baby. Yellow clothes would most certainly be for a boy!*" The driver pulled into Krasnoff's office parking lot where Jacob and her mother Doris were standing outside waiting for her. Jacob was talking fast the minute she got out of the car. "If you ever have any questions, Sophia, if you want to know how the child is doing, or if you want to update your contact information, just call me. I'll be your contact for any and all questions. Go home and get some rest."

He put her suitcase in Doris's trunk and gave the trunk a few taps to signal "all set to go." Mom got in the passenger's seat of the car, still silent and looking gaunt. Granny Doris tried to make small talk on the ride home. She was trying to avoid talking about the obvious loss in her daughter's heart. It was a common practice among southern women not to talk about things after they happened as if that made the whole thing go away. It never did of course, but rather buried all of those feelings a little deeper. Granny Doris told her stories of funny things Marilyn had done, and how excited Marilyn was going to be to see her mommy! *It was going to be wonderful to see Marilyn's smiling face again*, mom thought.

She was greeted at the door with giant hugs and pure joy in the fact she was home. Mom and Marilyn bonded so much more deeply over the next few years. It was as though mom took all of the love and attention that would have gone to the baby and poured it into loving my sister Marilyn. They continued to live there with Granny and Papa in Silk Hope.

Mom tried to keep the promise she made to her father about returning to school by trying her hand studying cosmetology. She excelled in her class for a while and was quite talented in making herself look good. She admitted she fell short on patience when it came to particularly demanding, catty women. She eventually dropped out of school and went to work at Levy's department store. That's where she was working when she saw her mother and father walking into Levy's together. She knew something was wrong because the two of them never went anywhere together. As they got closer to where she was standing her mother, unable to hold it in any longer, blurted it out: "William's been killed!" Mom fainted at the news. They brought her around with smelling salts and Papa drove her home.

William had become a helicopter pilot and was shot down in Vietnam in November of 1967. He was buried at Bonaventure Cemetery in Savannah with a full 21-gun salute and *Taps*. It was a terribly sad time for the whole family, especially for Peggy and their six children.

CHAPTER 6

They Meet

Mom loved to tell the story of how she left work at Levy's one evening and decided to meet her sister Peggy and some friends at a local Savannah spot. Duggar's lounge was on highway 17, the main road to everywhere. "The scenery and people passing through were constantly changing," she said. She continued telling me the story. She went inside and sat at a table, greeting everyone with laughter and jovial comments. The crowd was happy, and she said it was a nice relief from her having to be "on" at the department store all day. She did a quick scan to see who was there that night. Her eyes quickly fell on this tall handsome man with a head full of dark curly hair. He wore an open big collar button-down shirt revealing a just right hairy chest. Her gaze quickly darted away when his eyes made contact with hers. After a few moments of her absolutely ignoring this man was ever in the room, he made his way over to her table. "Would you like to dance?" he asked. "No thank you," she said. She turned away.

He turned and made his way back to his bar stool. A few moments later he watched as a much older man approached her to dance, and she danced with him. The tall man with dark curly hair mustered up more nerve to walk back over to the table asking her, "Why'd you tell me no, but you danced with that old guy?" He smiled at her.

"Because I wanted to dance with that old guy," she replied. There was a sarcastic grin on her face.

"Mind if I sit down?" he asked.

"It's a free country," she said. A devilish tone crept from her lips.

"What's your name?" he asked. He smiled and pulled up a chair.

"Honey," she said. "and yours?"

"Baby," he said. They both laughed as they continued this "I've known you forever" kind of banter back-and-forth. Her friends were all watching in amazement at how the two of them seemed to click. Ivy, her closest friend leaned over to whisper in her ear "Holy shit, Sophia! You're in trouble!"

"No, I'm not!" she replied. She was feeling way too smart to ever be tricked into what may appear to be relationship material again.

It was getting late so she began saying good night to everyone at the table, telling the man how nice it was to meet him. Perhaps they would cross paths again someday. "Well," he said, "I can be assured of that if you would be so kind as to give me your phone number."

She thought about it for a moment and wrote down a false number without a name. She turned and walked out the door with a girlish swing in her step and a huge smile on her face. He was right behind her, dancing around as she walked toward the car. He was trying to get some sort of commitment from her for a coffee date the very next day.

"Please, just meet me tomorrow for a cup of coffee, anywhere. You name the place and I will be there," he said.

She was amused by his persistence and said "Okay, I'll meet you at the Novelty bar on 16th street at Tybee Island tomorrow at 10 a.m."

"Are bars open at 10 a.m.?" he asked.

"They are at Tybee," she said. With that, she jumped in her car and headed to Peggy's house to relieve the babysitter. Peggy wanted to stay out and party a little longer.

She woke up early the next morning to get a jump start on getting ready for the coffee date. "OH!" It was then she realized the two of them never exchanged their real names. She laughed at the thought of having him at the table with all of them talking and dancing and not knowing his real name. She glanced outside and noticed Peggy's car wasn't there. She opened the door

and walked around the front and side of the house to
see if she parked anywhere else. No car, and after looking in Peggy's bedroom there was no Peggy, either. She
finished getting ready thinking surely her sister would
be home any time now. The closer the clock drew to
10 a.m. the more frustrated she became.

At 10:00 she called the Novelty bar where they
were supposed to meet. When the bartender answered,
mom said "Will you please ask out loud if there is a
'Baby' in there?"

The bartender said, "Sure, may I ask who is calling?"
"Yes," she said. "It's Honey."

The bartender thought it was a prank call and
hung up the phone. So, she called her right back and
explained that they had just met the night before, and
never exchanged real names. So, the bartender bit, and
said loud and clear, "Is there someone named Baby
here?" Mom said she could hear him in the background
saying, "Right here, right here, here I am," he said.
He reached for the phone. Her frustration turned to
laughter. She started to explain that she wasn't going
to be able to make it down to meet him because her
sister wasn't home yet. He wouldn't accept that for an
instant. He told her he would wait there as long as
it took, all day if he needed to. She couldn't get over
how determined he was to see her again. She told him
she would drive down when her sister got home. She
finally arrived around 1:00 p.m.

Joseph was his name. They shared lunch together
and talked for hours. He told her how life was on the

eighty cow dairy farm where he grew up in Minnesota. He had six older sisters and one older brother, making him the baby boy. Only one sister was younger than him, and her name was June. He had been an all-star athlete in high school playing football, basketball, and baseball - and he ran track too. He had the most practice running because every day he had to run home from school to do chores, then he'd run back to school for practice. Farm life was hard, but if they wanted to play sports they did what they had to do. He said he had to do that, sometimes in the absolute coldest weather you can imagine. She shivered listening to him having no experience at all with cold weather.

"If it gets in the '30s here we're all in an uproar worrying about the pipes freezing," she said. He just shook his head, saying, "Try 30-below!" After high school, he went to St. Cloud State University where he played football and basketball for a year. He and college life didn't work out he admitted. He was getting into a little trouble so he decided to move to Oregon and go to work with his uncle Bob at a lumber company. He worked there for about three years, but when he figured out there wasn't a lot going on in Oregon he decided to enlist in the Army and was stationed in Germany. His assignment was playing sports. He tried his hand at umpiring baseball a little while he was over there. That's where he met a man who became a dear friend and mentor named Bobby Dearie. Bobby told him if he ever wanted to think about umpiring as a career to give him a call down in Daytona, Florida.

"I was discharged in 1967. It was 40 below in Minnesota and 75 in Daytona, and here I am," he said. He smiled. She smiled back at him feeling as though she could have sat there all day listening to him talk about school, sports, family, and the farm. She asked if he'd like to walk down to the beach. They left their shoes in the Novelty bar and walked one block down 16th street to where it dead-ended on the beach. It was there he spun her around with a hand on her shoulder and gave her a simple sweet kiss. They walked, talked, laughed, and drew things in the sand.

It had been a perfect date she thought. She inhaled deeply preparing to say goodbye. This time she gave him her real phone number and name.

The very next day the phone rang, and she knew it would be him before she ever picked up the receiver. Her heart was racing, but why? She wasn't about to let any kind of crazy thing happen between them. So she did some self-talk that sounded something like this: *Just allow yourself to enjoy this time, know that you are not going to let it become serious, and just have some fun, some much needed fun.*

She answered the phone in the best "phone voice" she could conjure up. "Hello," he said. "Is Honey there?" They laughed. "I was wondering if you might like to come to Grayson Stadium tonight for a ballgame. You can watch the game and bring a friend if you'd like. We can all go for coffee afterward."

"Sure," she said, "that sounds great."

"I'll leave two tickets at will-call for you and your friend. See you soon, Sophia, Honey." She laughed and hung up the phone just long enough to call Ivy. "You won't believe who just called me for another date," she said. "Oh yes I will," said Ivy.

"He invited me to a game at Grayson Stadium tonight. He said to bring a friend. Are you up for it?"

"Sure," said Ivy. "I'll pick you up."

They both showed up at the stadium looking like they belonged anywhere BUT Savannah, Georgia. They were both unusually tall and very well proportioned. Ivy had long, beautiful red hair, and Sophia was still blonde. They were dressed to the nines. They enjoyed watching Joseph call the game and afterward, they all went to Johnny Harris for dinner and drinks. They shared lively stories of years gone by. Sophia and Ivy shared how life was growing up in the neighborhood of Silk Hope, and Joseph shared his life as an umpire. The conversations flowed like wine, and the night flew by. They all said goodbyes in the parking lot. Joseph asked mom if it would be alright if he called her again.

"I suppose that would be okay," she said. It was a very girlish, eyelash batting kind of way. "ERRR," she said after getting in the car with Ivy. "Why do I act like that with him?" To which Ivy just laughed. "I told you, trouble. I knew it at Duggar's, the night y'all met," she said. They both laughed again.

It was rather late when she got home, so she tried to dial down her excitement and enter the house quietly. Opening the door she found her father sitting there in his easy chair. "Good evening, young lady. Want to tell me what it is you're doing?" "Hi, daddy," she said. She tried to be serious. "I got asked to go to a ballgame at Grayson Stadium from an umpire who is traveling through. So Ivy and I went to the game, then he took us out for a nice dinner and drinks at Johnny Harris. Sorry, I'm so late getting in. Time just flew by."

Her father could already tell by the tone of her voice and her body language that this wasn't just any guy. "So, tell me about him," he said.

"Okay," she said. "He was raised on a dairy farm in Minnesota, and he played football in the Army. While he was stationed in Germany he met someone who said to call him down in Florida and talk to him if he was ever interested in umpiring as a career. So he got back to Minnesota where it was 40 degrees below zero, looked at the weather to see it was 75 and sunny in Florida, and the rest is history," she said.

Giggling with a bit of a buzz from the cocktails and amazed at how well she had retained all of what he shared with her she thought *Maybe I AM in trouble!* The thought brought a smile to her face.

"He does sound interesting indeed, but you know nobody dates my daughter without me knowing them first or at least meeting them," her father said.

"Daddy," she said. "I'm almost twenty-three years old! I've already been married and divorced with a child."

"I don't care," he said. "My house, my rules. Invite him here before you see him again." He spat his chewing tobacco plug in the brass spittoon beside his chair and left for bed. *No way was she going to put Joseph through that!* she thought. Her daddy could embarrass the fool out of her. He could scare the living daylights out of anyone who dared look at her inappropriately. *I can't believe he's treating me like a child* she thought. She tiptoed in to snuggle with Marilyn for the night.

It was several days before Joseph called again. He drove from town to town calling games, sometimes sleeping in the car. It wasn't unusual for the guys to give pay phone numbers as their own and park beside the booth to jump out and answer the phone when it rang. My mother would never know of these poor house stories. He pretended to have it all together when he talked to her. It was as though they hadn't missed a moment when he called. They talked like they'd known one another for years. The chemistry between them was building each time they spoke. Joseph told her he would be in town the following weekend and would love to take her out on a date. "Well yes," she said. "There's just one catch. You have to come to meet my mother, father, and daughter Marilyn. My daddy is really old-fashioned in a southern kind of way. So if you're willing to do that you have a date."

"Sure," he said without hesitation. "I would love to meet your family. Let's get together next weekend. Tell me a little bit about your parents Sophia." he said.

"My daddy is a retired boxer with a mean right hook, and my mother works at St. Joseph's hospital so you're covered," she said. She roared with laughter.

Joseph didn't laugh quite as hard with the mental image he had of being knocked out by her father and taken to the hospital. "No, really," she continued, "he was a boxer, and now he sells and delivers furniture for his brother. Mom works the switchboard at Saint Joseph's hospital. Marilyn is a beautiful bundle of joy. She's five years old. She loves adventure, any and all kinds of critters. She's a very independent child who wants things the way she wants them and has been known to throw a tantrum when life doesn't go her way."

"That's a great description of everyone," he said. "Now I know what I'm in for. I look forward to seeing you all soon."

She hung up the phone and asked her mother, "Will you pinch me? This guy just doesn't seem real. He seems too good to be true. He's coming here to meet you all next weekend."

"Really!" said Granny Doris. "I can't wait. Whatever will I wear?" Mom was excited too, but she secretly harbored some fear about becoming involved again, especially with a man so incredibly handsome and smooth. She said this man would "give the Kennedys a run for their money." He was that slick, but she did love his persistence in courting her.

Joseph came to her house the next weekend with some chewing tobacco for Papa James. He had a new cookbook for Granny Doris, a butterfly net for Marilyn, and some flowers for mom. He was an instant hit with everyone in the house! He told farming stories and stories of Germany with mom's father James. He put an apron on and helped her mother wash dishes in the kitchen after dinner and told Marilyn a bedtime story of the lake monster that lived in Minnesota. By the time Joseph left the Wilsons were all but planning a wedding! Mom said she walked him out to his car to say goodnight, with one sweet simple kiss. He looked into her eyes for what seemed like forever. Then he got into his car and drove away. She just stood there feeling the warm humid air on her skin, listening to the orchestra of crickets singing in the night. With a sky full of brilliant stars, and the warm sand beneath her feet, she enjoyed what was a most magical, mystical moment.

As the days, weeks, and months flew by their friendship grew to be more and more. She would always avoid his persistence when it came to sharing herself with him. It had been about seven months since they met. He was indeed a patient man. She tried to keep it light, even though the desire to know him in "that way" was getting harder and harder for her to resist. She knew to take that step with him meant going to another level, and she wasn't sure she was quite ready.

As a native of Minnesota, Joseph's experience with the ocean wasn't much. He'd heard mom talk about crabbing and thought he might like to give it a try. So one afternoon he stopped by to pick her up, and they drove down to the creek. They had crabbing baskets, chicken necks for bait, and a five-gallon bucket to collect the harvest. She showed him how to rig the baskets with a piece of chicken tied inside the center of the basket, and how to tie a heavy sinker on the bottom of the basket to keep the tide current from pulling the basket from the bottom of the creek. The trap basket would need to lie flat on the creek floor. Next came instructions on how to pull the basket up ever so slowly so the crab doesn't get spooked, and scurry. He pulled up the first basket that had been down for about five minutes. With all of the excitement and enthusiasm of a child he shouted, "LOOK! I HAVE ONE!!" She rushed over to see his catch and began to laugh uncontrollably. It was a baby crab that wouldn't even cover the palm of your hand.

"One thing's for sure," she said through her laughter. "Those Minnesota boys know NOTHING about catching a blue crab." Her laughter was quite bruising to his masculinity. He acted out by throwing the basket down on the dock saying, "Screw it then! I'm over this crabbing shit! Who likes to eat those bottom-sucking scavengers anyway?"

Mom said she could tell his ego was smashed so she went to him. She was still laughing. She gave him a hug and added, "Aww c'mon, you gotta be able to laugh at yourself. It's all in good fun. It's okay, baby," she said. She ran her hands through his curls.

One thing led to another as all of her defenses were gone. They enjoyed one another completely right there on the banks of the salty creek. Both of them collapsed in perfect solitude in one another's arms. She knew now that this bridge had been crossed, there would be no turning back. It was a time and place of love blossoming. The kind of love that time never steals. Its roots run deep, devoured by the bliss of each and every moment. They were consumed by continuous thoughts of each other, with each of those thoughts bringing rise to a smile that wouldn't go away. It was a love so true they wished the whole world could feel the way they were feeling. Surely it was a connection made in heaven and only by grace had it fallen upon them. They were in the grasp of love's bliss, taking any and every opportunity to enjoy one another as fully and completely as they could. She told stories of them pulling over on the side of the road or running into cornfields. Her stories were always full of romance, adventure, and LOTS of passion. It seemed they were a match made in heaven. They made plans to marry, have a house full of babies, and love this way forever. As it seemed to happen with mom, the "having babies" part came first. It was no surprise to her as much as they had been together.

Joseph's reaction to the news that she may be pregnant was bittersweet. He wanted to do it all, but not in this order. He confided to a friend in Minnesota who encouraged him to "do the right thing." Joseph decided to take his friend's advice. It was a huge risk to take coming from a devout Roman Catholic family and marrying a Baptist girl from down south! Mom agreed to study catechism and change religions for him. Still, marriages of different faiths were frowned upon by church and family. The surprise announcement to mom's side of the family was very well received. Her parents had never been more pleased to hear the news. She always joked that they loved Joseph more than they did her.

Joseph didn't have a lot of money, and she had none. They opted for a quick ceremony at the courthouse. They would use the money they did have to rent an apartment and buy some furniture. After all, their love was sufficient for the two of them. Neither of them felt they required a lavish ceremony to prove it to anyone else. She was satisfied, very happy, and was so excited to start her new life with Marilyn and Joseph. She had so much fun decorating their apartment with Ivy's help. With the all too popular animal print decor, it looked very chic, exotic, and of course ready for entertaining!

Joseph planned a trip for the three of them to go to Minnesota over his next break. Joseph's dad Howard had long stopped farming and lived with his second wife Pearl in a small house on a hilltop in St. Anthony, Minnesota. The newlyweds and Marilyn traveled to one of his sister's dairy farms where Mom and Marilyn both learned how to milk a cow by hand. Joseph's sister Julia invited them inside the house to enjoy some homemade banana-nut bread and butter.

When she and Joseph's baby sister June had a chance to chat privately for a while June told mom that their birth mother had passed away from a heart attack when Joseph was just fourteen years old. He was the baby boy of the family, and he and their mother were very close. They couldn't get him to come down off the roof of the house after he was told of her passing. Then on top of that, he had a high school girlfriend who passed away too. June thought the loss was more than he could handle, so he started acting out.

"He just got into a lot of trouble," she said. "He wrecked a couple of cars drinking and driving. He could have bled to death after one of those accidents if it hadn't been so cold outside. He had to crawl to a house far away in the middle of the night for help while bleeding severely with injuries. He became very stubborn, and rebellious. Our dad talked him into going to live with Uncle Bob in Oregon to work with him at the lumber business. Then he joined the Army and got lucky, landing a spot on the Army football team. It was like he had guardian angels everywhere. Maybe it was our mother and that girlfriend of his watching out for him from up above."

"Maybe so," mom said.

She thanked her for sharing all of that with her and thanked Julia for having them out to her farm. It was a beautiful piece of country and the Gartman family was strong. Everyone fell in love with mom and my sister Marilyn. They loved to sit and listen to their southern accents when they spoke. They were welcomed into the family, Baptist and all. Mom and Marilyn enjoyed the celebrations with their new relatives, and they all danced so well. Joseph's dad Howard gave them a two thousand dollar check as a wedding gift. Mom said she watched in amazement as he danced the polka, and said to herself, "I think this Catholic way of life will suit me just fine. When did having a drink and dancing become so sinful anyway?"

Mom was so excited to be having Joseph's baby but in quiet times feeling the growing child inside her brought back memories of the last pregnancy. She wondered, *How is my baby doing now? How's my boy? Are they loving him as I would? I wish I could have him here with Marilyn, Joseph, and this baby. We would all be so happy.*

She decided to reach out to Jacob Krasnoff. He told her she could call him anytime. The receptionist put her right through to him.

"Hello, Jacob," she said. "You told me I could call you anytime and update my contact information and check on the welfare of my baby. I'm married now, and we're living here in Savannah on White Bluff Road in some nice apartments.

"Oh," said Jacob, "that's a very nice area of town Sophia. What does your husband do?"

"He's a baseball umpire with the Southern League, and he also roofs with Bonnets Better Roofing Company. We would be able to provide for my child if anything ever happened with that nice Christian couple."

"I see," said Jacob. "I'll update your information, Sophia. The child is fine, very well cared for, and loved as promised. Now you take care of yourself. Thank you for calling." He hung up the phone.

Mom sat there with the receiver held close to her heart, tears rolling down her cheeks. Joseph walked in at that very moment. He asked "What's wrong, darling? Has something happened to someone?" He wrapped his strong arms around her and held her close while she cried.

She said she was tired of holding this secret. She told him she loved him so much, but feared being judged or even worse, abandoned if she told him. "I must share something with you. It's a deep hurt, but you must promise me you won't think differently of me. You won't judge me."

"Dear God, Sophia," he said, "Have you killed someone?" Laughing through tears she said, "No silly man!"

"Anything else I can take then," he said. She shared the whole story with him, and he held her close, knowing and seeing how much she loved children, how adoring she was with Marilyn, and the way she spoke of her nieces and nephews. He could only imagine how difficult a time this must have been for her and still was. It was never brought up again, but she felt so relieved having told him. She never was one for secrets, and telling him seemed to free her in a lot of ways.

Her checkups with Dr. Angel were going well. "This baby is really growing," he said. "You're losing weight, but I'm not worried about it. This baby is taking all of what you're eating, that's all."

She craved watermelon more than anything with this pregnancy, so all summer long she swam in the pool and ate watermelon. "According to the heart rate, I'm guessing this is going to be a big baby boy!" the doctor said.

"Really!" she said. "Joseph will be so happy. I can't wait to tell him." "It's not 100% reliable but pretty close," said Dr. Angel. The pregnancy had reached the point where Joseph would be able to feel him move too. "Thank you, Dr. Angel, you really are an Angel!" she said. She smiled at him.

Early September came quickly. Mom's baby belly was large enough now that people were asking if she was having twins. "No," she would reply. "Just one big, healthy boy." Joseph was amazed looking at her now, at how pregnant she was at full term. He thought she was more beautiful than ever. They rushed home for some time alone before Marilyn came home from dance class. While they were making love, a big warm gush came and covered them both. "What was that?" he exclaimed, half terrified.

"Oh, my water broke!" she said. We've got to go to the hospital."

"Okay-Okay," he said. He ran around the house nervously. Nothing was prepared. *The baby wasn't supposed to come for another three weeks*, so she called the neighbor who Marilyn was carpooling with to see if she could stay with her until Granny Doris could get there to pick her up. Joseph had the hospital bag and the keys, and out the door he ran. She laughed at his nervousness in between contractions. "You might want to put some pants on," she said. She laughed even harder. He looked down to reveal red boxer shorts, socks, and shoes.

Dr. Angel met them at St. Joseph's Hospital. He said Joseph could stay in the room with her until the contractions became unbearably painful. They would then put her out and deliver the baby. *This must be the same technique they used in Jesup* she thought, remembering the last labor once again. Joseph and Dr. Angel were telling baseball stories and jokes. Sister Josetta was there to help with the delivery. She and Granny Doris had become good friends, getting to know one another very well when Granny Doris took the job as a switchboard operator at the hospital. Sister Josetta said, "This baby is going to be a professional swimmer. I have never seen so much water as it continued to break." When the pain became unbearable, Dr. Angel asked Joseph to leave the room. Mom woke up to meet a 10-pound 1-ounce baby girl! That was me!

"A girl?" she said. "A big girl," said dad. He carried me over to meet my mother face- to- face. "Dear God, she looks like you, Joseph," she said. "We have so many boy things to return. What will we name her? Joseph Chance is not going to work anymore," she said. She smiled.

"How about Honey? Remember when we first met and I told you that was my name?" she asked.

"Yes, I remember," he said. "I told you mine was Baby. You want to name her Honey Baby?" he said. They laughed. "Don't make me laugh!" she said. She held her lower abdomen trying to cushion it from pain when she shook with laughter. "Josetta is the feminine name for Joseph in Italy," said Sister Josetta with a smile.

She'd been there with Dr. Angel throughout the entire labor and delivery. "How about we name her

Honey Josetta since Honey was my name when we met and Josetta is the feminine version of Joseph? Part of me, part of you?" Mom asked.

"Okay," he said. "Honey Josetta it is."

Mom's parents, my granny and papa, along with my big sister Marilyn were allowed to come into the hospital room to visit. This baby girl is stirring things up around here," said Granny Doris. She's the record holder as the biggest baby girl here at the new St Joseph's. Everyone was oohing and ahhing over the extra large baby that I was. Everyone except my sister Marilyn. Mom was careful about her feelings, especially since she'd been the only one for seven years. She read books on how important it would be to let someone other than her carry the new baby into the house for the first time. How to make being a big sister a big deal. She remained concerned as she noticed Marilyn never really got excited when they talked about me. Sure enough, her concerns were realized when she caught her trying to tip my bassinet over and dump me out. She wanted to get rid of this little thing that was stealing all of her attention. Not just from our mother, but from everyone! Doris our granny would be the one to answer the call for more TLC where Marilyn was concerned. She'd been so close with Marilyn because they lived with her off and on from the time of the divorce from Marilyn's father Charles until the marriage with Joseph. The bond Marilyn and Granny Doris already shared would continue to grow stronger and stronger over the years.

CHAPTER 7

Big Leagues

The day after my second birthday is when my dad got the call. It's not often an umpire gets called up to the big leagues. There are so few of them. Someone has to retire, get fired, or die for that space to open. It happened. He got the call. He hurried home to share the news with us. It all seemed so surreal to him. His mind was going over all of the changes this meant for our lives. His driving days would be over. Now he would be flying to these cities all over the U.S and Canada! He would be on television! He would finally be able to provide for us the way he wanted to. Mom could have a decorating budget. He got more and more excited to tell her on the drive home. He burst through the door with enough energy to spook her in the kitchen. She jumped with a quick "OH! - What is it?" He began to dance around the kitchen. "Big Leagues Baby, Big Leagues! I've been called up!"

"Oh, Joe! That's great news!" she said. He picked her up and spun her around the room. Marilyn, who walked in the kitchen late didn't understand what was happening. She did understand that everyone was happy about whatever it was, so she began to dance right along with them.

Dad flew to New York to the American League office that next week to sign contracts, get health insurance info from HR, get set up for a physical, measured for uniforms, and shoes. He'd instructed my mother to search for a house for them in the best school district for Marilyn. He told her to be certain to search for crime rates also. If he was going to be traveling most of the time he wanted the peace of mind that we were all safe. She found a house she loved on Bull Street in downtown Savannah. We could visit local parks and museums. The Savannah beach, better known as Tybee Island and Fort Pulaski were only a twenty minute drive away. Life was good, and we were happy.

Mom said they did a lot of entertaining at the new house. Friends and other umpires dad worked with came over frequently with their wives for delicious meals that she took the time to research and prepare. She loved to cook and entertain. Drinks and jokes flowed freely, the two of them played off of one another so well. They were a magnetic couple that others loved to be around.

March rolled around much faster than either of them had anticipated. It was time for spring training down in Florida. They marked the calendar together with the dates they would be seeing one another. She could drive to Florida easily enough. If he were working anywhere else she would just have to wait. The thought of it saddened her, so she tried not to think of it. Saying goodbye was much harder than they thought it would be. For mom it was as though the empty feeling of loss and abandonment had returned for her. Insecurities began to surface in her mind. She remembered Charles traveling for his job and having been lied to. She began to become consumed with thoughts like, *"What will he do with his downtime while he is on the road? Will he be going to nightclubs and bars with the guys? He'll be living the high life while I'm here cooking and cleaning with the babies!"*

They talked to each other every night for the first week. Dad was eager to share all of his experiences, and the people he was meeting. She loved to hear the happiness in his voice as he went through all the details. The following week's calls were less frequent, but the conversations were comforting and fulfilling to them both. He called one day and told her to get her mother to take her down to the Backus/Cadillac/Pontiac dealership in Savannah, there was something there waiting for her.

"Really? A surprise?" Grinning from ear to ear, she hurried off the phone to call her mother for a ride. She arrived to find a big, beautiful, silver Pontiac. This thing was huge. Big enough to load up all of us children, hers and our Aunt Peggy's! We could all have some adventurous excursions. Eight-track player, leather. This car had the works. The first trip she planned to make was down to sunny Florida to see him! They'd been apart for almost a month. She said she had that same giddy "butterflies" feeling she had when they first met. Mom's sister aunt Peggy agreed to let Marilyn stay at her house to play with her cousins for the weekend. Granny Doris and Papa James watched me.

The drive to Florida seemed to take forever, but she said the time started to move quickly the minute they were in each other's arms again. What a wonderful weekend they had! Mom got to meet some of the crew of umpires he would be working with all year, along with some of their wives. They had a lush hotel room, with a huge outdoor pool. Mom loved to swim. She was amused to find out that my dad couldn't swim. She was lying beside the pool admiring the professional-looking long strokes he was making with his arms. She stood to join him in the pool, and that's when she noticed he was walking along the bottom rather than swimming. She laughed so hard, but recalling the "crabbing" gig she remembered that his ego couldn't handle that kind of embarrassment. He made her promise not to tell anyone he couldn't swim. He was so muscular and solid. He went straight to the bottom every time he tried. The time in each other's company and arms was wonderful but passed all too fast. The weekend was over before she knew it. She packed up the Pontiac she had affectionately named Bertha and headed back to Savannah.

Back at home she got involved with helping Aunt Peggy decorate her big two-story home on Whitemarsh Island, a small island community on the way to Tybee Island. Her niece Sarah had her first bedroom all to herself. Mom painted a huge Alice in Wonderland mural on one of the walls. It was so magical. To see it made you feel like you were really there. Her artistic talents were many. She could draw, paint, and write so well. All of the reader's senses came to life in the descriptions of her words. She never wanted to sell any of her paintings, and she stored countless half-written manuscripts under the bed. Nobody knew why she wasn't a famous writer, but all who read anything she had done agreed she should've been.

Mom knew summer break was just around the corner so she asked Peggy if it would be all right if she took her kids to Disney World with us. She knew they'd never experienced anything like that before and knew it would give her sister a much needed break. Mom called dad as soon as she got home from Peggy's to tell him how the mural turned out in Sarah's room and asked if she could take Peggy's kids, Marilyn, and me to Disney.

"Do you think it will be too expensive Joe?" she asked.

"Not at all," he said. "Take them! That's why we bought that big car! I'm so glad you are enjoying your family, Sophia," he said. They both agreed they couldn't wait to be in one another's arms again, and they said goodnight.

My mother was just as excited about Disney as all of the children were. She had the same sense of adventure and imagination as the kids did. They loaded up all of our things in big ole Bertha, and we hit the road. They sang songs, played I spy, and a host of other car games to keep the four hour ride to Orlando interesting. The children had experiences of a lifetime on that trip with Nana. They respected her, so they listened when she told them they had to eat their vegetables, and she often corrected their behavior and grammar. They didn't mind the corrections because she was so much fun to be with. The trip was a success, but she was glad to get back home where she could get some rest.

As soon as she walked in the door she made a phone call to dad's hotel room in Boston. She didn't have the game schedule, so she decided to leave a message with the operator at the hotel desk. "Please have Joseph call home when he gets in for some news, some good news." The front desk operator validated what she heard and said the message would be delivered. We all had dinner, and mom put me and Marilyn in a big bubble bath with extra bubbles and tucked us in with a "good night moon" story. *It's strange not to have heard from him by now* she thought. *Maybe the operator didn't give him the message.* So she called again to ring his room at 9:30. Still no answer. She decided to take a bath herself, thinking maybe it was a late game, and they were out to eat or something. She tried again at 11; no answer. She began to call every half hour, then every fifteen minutes becoming completely obsessive until at 3 o'clock in the morning she fell into an exhausted sleep across the bed with the phone beside her. Marilyn woke her up at 8 a.m. with a stray kitty she found in the backyard.

"Oh, Marilyn," mom said, "let's put the kitty back outside so it can find its mama, okay? Then we can have some breakfast." She poured Marilyn a bowl of cereal and sat across the table from her just looking into her big, beautiful eyes. "What a beautiful child!" she said to her. She had a big smile on her face. "Mama is going to rest for a little bit while Honey is still sleeping. When we get up we'll go shopping and find something fun at the toy store. How does that sound?"

"Yes!" Marilyn said. "Can I hold the kitty until then?"

"No honey, we have to let the kitty stay outside. Joseph doesn't like them in the house."

"Okayyyy," she said. She was disappointed. "I can bring them in at granny's house," she said.

Mom always said dad liked for things to be extra clean. It seemed to be worse the longer he was away. Mom always thought he liked and expected the house should always look like a freshly cleaned hotel room with everything in its place. Lived-in houses rarely looked like that, but there was no convincing him of that. If something was left undone he would do it himself when he got home. She ended up living how she wanted to while he was on the road. Then she quickly made everything the way he would expect before he came home.

This didn't make for an easy relationship between him and little Marilyn though. It kind of made him seem like the villain to her. The house rules changed completely when he came home and not for the better in her eyes. She was really tired of all of the fuss about this new sister too. Everyone was happy about it except her. She wanted her mama all to herself, and she was mad about having to share.

Finally around 2 p.m., the phone rang. It was him. He was trying to make light of not being in his room all night, but he could feel the chill through the phone line. To hear mom tell it, she didn't say a word. She just listened.

"Richard got really drunk during and after dinner, so much so he couldn't even walk. So I helped him back to his hotel room. I kind of had to help him out ya know. He got sick and all. He slept on his bathroom floor sick like that all night. I didn't want to leave him alone like that, so I just laid across his bed and fell asleep. He's quite humble today. Don't say anything to his wife Cindy if y'all talk, I'm sure he wouldn't want her to know how wasted he was. We gotta look out for one another out here sometimes honey. Each other is all we have on the road. I'm sorry you were worried."

Mom said she had a queasy feeling in her gut. *Yuk! What is that feeling?* Maybe nerves, maybe because she hadn't eaten. "Okay Mr. Joseph Gartman," she said to him, "I'm buying your story this time, but don't ever do that to me again! Tell Richard he better learn how to hold his booze, or he'll have me to deal with!" she said.

"What's the news honey? I have a message here from the hotel. You have news for me," he asked.

"Yes I did, but I've forgotten what was so important now," she said. "I miss you so much."

He replied, "Only ten days till next break. I'll be home before you know it."

She said her stomach still didn't feel quite right. She got something to eat and took a shower and started feeling a little bit better. She decided to keep the promise she made to Marilyn and go to the toy store. Perhaps she would find some things for the house, too. They finished shopping early and decided at the last minute to drive out to Silk Hope to see granny and Papa. She always said she could feel the tension leave her body as soon as she entered the drive. *This home was her safe place,* she thought. She could always find peace here. Her parents were surprised by the spontaneous visit but loved that we were all there. Papa had been fishing that day, and her mother was frying up those fresh redbreast fish to be enjoyed with a big pot of grits and some fried lace cornbread. They got all caught up on the events in each other's lives. Papa, looking at the TV guide, announced aloud that dad would be calling a game aired on television in a few days, and he would love it if they could all get together to watch it. "When the announcers introduce the umpires, Joseph always reaches up to tip his hat," Papa said. "That is a big hello to everyone watching at home. He told me that himself," he said. He was gleaming with pride for the accomplishments his son-in-law had made in his career. Mom agreed that we should all get together for the game. She gathered our things and loaded up the car to drive back home for the night. Both Marilyn and I were asleep when we arrived. She carried me into the crib and went back out to get Marilyn from the large back seat where she lay with the stuffed lizard she'd chosen at the toy store. *She was really getting too big to carry* mom thought. She grew more and more beautiful by the day. *Marilyn was named after her father's favorite actress, and if her beauty continued at this rate, she too would be gracing the silver screen,* was all my mom could think as she tucked her in for the night. Snug as a bug in a rug. "Sweet dreams," she whispered. She kissed her on the forehead and turned out the light.

The next week and a half flew by as mom prepared the house and the kitchen for dad's few days off at home. He ate at some of the finest restaurants in the states, but he was tired of that. He loved coming home to her good home cooking. We all met him at the airport with welcome home hugs. Mom said time seemed to be a whirlwind of loving, talking, cooking, and cleaning. Those were the fastest two days in the world she remembered as they drove back to the airport for his next flight out. It was always hard for her to take him to the airport. Now she preferred to just drop him off, as going inside and watching him walk away always made her cry. She told herself that the baseball season's end was near. She would have him home, all to herself for the holidays.

The next day as she was picking up the house a little bit, she noticed a book beside the chair in their bedroom where Joseph left his suitcase. *"What is this?"* she asked herself. She bent over to pick it up. It was a black book, very well worn and tattered. She opened it but really wished she hadn't. *I remember this,* she thought as she went back in her memory to when he'd first shown it to her.

"Look Sophia," he said, showing her the book full of names. "I've played the field. I've had more than my share of women. Now all I want is you."

She smiled slightly with the memory. *Why am I finding this now? Why is he still carrying it?* she wondered. She thumbed through the pages of what seemed to be hundreds of women. There was some kind of side note that appeared to be a grading system. Her mind immediately went back to the night he wasn't in his room. That same sick feeling began to fill her lower gut again. So strong was the feeling this time that she actually ran to the toilet to throw up.

Wiping her face with a cool washcloth, she sat in the bedroom chair with the book in hand, wondering what to do. Her mind began to "try on" different scenarios. *Do I need to call these women? Do I call Joseph? How could I have fallen so deeply for this man? I knew he was way too slick when I met him. I knew women would be drawn to him, just like I was. Who was I kidding?*

Myself obviously. Maybe I'll just hide the book and wait to see if he asks for it.

Unable to decide which course of action to take she decided just to sit with it and do nothing until she had a clear mind. That didn't work either. The longer she sat there the worse it got.

She decided to call her best friend Ivy. She always seemed to have strong, logical advice. She answered and listened diligently to mom's story along with all of the thoughts of what it could mean running through her mind. Ivy calmly said "Sophia you're going to drive yourself crazy with this. You should call him to see what he has to say."

Sophia finally decided to take Ivy's advice, but not tonight. She was far too tired from the endless mental chatter. She decided to wait and called him the next day.

The phone rang in his hotel room the next morning. "Hey baby," he answered. He was glad to hear from her.

"How are you, Joseph?" He could hear the wrath in her voice.

"I'm just fine. What's up?"

"Are you missing anything?" she asked him.

"Only you, baby. I'm only missing you," he said. "Are you okay Sophia?"

"Well I was okay until I found your little black book while cleaning yesterday," she said. Her voice was becoming more and more stern and unforgiving. She heard a lighthearted chuckle from him. "What's so damn funny?" she asked.

"You are!" he exclaimed. "Why are you snooping around in my stuff anyway?" he asked.

"I wasn't snooping. It was laid out here on our bedroom floor, so I picked it up. Who are all of these women, Joseph?"

"Sophia," he said, "this may come as a shock to you, but I wasn't a virgin when we met." He was trying to make her laugh, but it wasn't working. "I've had that book since I was 18 years old! I enjoyed my youth, darling. That was then this is now. Put it away," he said.

"Even if what you're saying is all true I don't like the way you grade them along with side notes so you don't mix them up! I mean REALLY?!"

"It's okay baby. You know why?" he asked.

"No, tell me why."

"Because you're Number One, and you'll always be Number One. Don't worry so much my love. I love you. Gotta run, we're going to get some grub. Give Marilyn and Honey Jo a kiss for me," he said.

"I love you too," she said. She felt foolish for the way she reacted.

She called Ivy back to thank her for the good advice. She explained everything as Joseph had to her.

"See there," Ivy said. "You wasted all of that energy and got no sleep over a book from the past."

"Yeah, I guess so," she said. "Thanks again for being such a dear friend, Ivy. I'll talk with you later."

Finally the time came for dad to come home for a while before going to the Dominican Republic to call winter ball there. Mom said she meant to look and feel her best when picking him up from the airport. She took a long relaxing bath and shaved her legs. She rolled her long blonde hair on the heat rollers and used a magazine photo to copy the cat eye makeup technique. She wore her favorite blue jeans and a beautiful fall lightweight sweater. She finished the look with tall boots and a leopard-print handbag.

Dad was delighted to see her looking so incredibly fit and put together. She begged him not to rush straight home. She knew he had his fill of the nightlife and eating out while he was on the road, but she felt she never got to have that kind of downtime with him. She had pre-arranged for granny Doris to keep us kids for the night. He couldn't resist her heartfelt plea for a night on the town. The two of them went to Savannah's River Street. They had dinner at the Boars Head restaurant, and they bar-hopped up and down River Street. They got a hotel room right there on the riverfront and made love like they did when they first met until they collapsed into an exhausted sleep. The time together was so perfect he asked her if she would join him in the Dominican for the month of December through the New Year. She was excited. It would be her first trip out of the country.

Marilyn was in school, and the trip would require her to miss too much time, so she couldn't go. Granny Doris urged mom to go. She and Papa would love to have Marilyn for the holidays and would be happy to get her back-and-forth to school. Mom agreed and decided that she and dad would host Thanksgiving for everyone since they wouldn't be around for Christmas and the New Year. They invited Granny, Papa, Uncle Earnest, and Aunt Margie. Dad cooked a huge turkey and a ham. Mom made all of the southern trimmings, homemade mashed potatoes with bacon gravy, sweet potato casserole, and Oyster dressing. She also made biscuits, Pecan pie, and Banana pudding. It was a lovely time shared by all.

Mom had a glorious time in the Dominican Republic. She was greeted by a young lady named Nancy who was staying at the hotel with them. Nancy was a Chilean woman with beautiful dark skin. Mom said she couldn't help but notice that Nancy had a servant lady who waited on her hand and foot. She laid out her clothes and even brushed her hair for her. Nancy invited mom to her beach house. When mom couldn't figure out why Nancy had a house and was staying at the hotel. She asked dad about the woman. He said she was one of the other umpire's girlfriends.

She took Nancy up on the offer to go to the beach house and was amazed at the differences of coastal homes in the United States versus the Dominican. There weren't a lot of fancy houses there. They were quite simple, humble homes with old furnishings. The beaches were mostly rocks, and the soup that was served to them for lunch had a chicken foot in it. Mom said she politely turned down the simmering bowl unable to get past the protruding foot. She was amazed there were no real Christmas trees. They simply had bare branches decorated with beautiful ornaments hung all over them. Many were made from coral or the petrified amber that divers brought up from beneath the sea. Artisans handcrafted many beautiful things from it.

Felipe was a shoeshine boy mom made fast friends with. Every time she walked out of the hotel there he sat asking if he could polish my baby shoes again. He dressed in a nice pair of shorts and a pressed white cotton shirt. He opened a piece of folded foil to reveal some beautiful delicate homemade cookies his mother made for us. Felipe had gone to school long enough to learn to read and write. He had to quit when his mother could no longer afford to send him, so, he shined shoes to help the family survive. He became my mom's sidekick. When she went to the market or shopping he went with her to negotiate and make sure she wasn't taken advantage of. Dad tipped him abundantly during our stay.

All of the umpires and their wives or dates were invited to the U.S. Embassy for a New Year's Eve celebration. It was a beautiful way to end the month long stay. Dad took us to the airport the following day. He would stay behind long enough to finish out the season and have time to come home for a short time before leaving again for spring training in the states.

The first night that they were apart Mom had a dream that he was with another woman. The images were so vivid and real. She awoke drenched in sweat and trembling all over. Needing to hear his voice and feel the reassurance, she called his hotel at 2 a.m. No answer. Wondering if he might be sleeping hard, she called over and over again, but still no answer. She walked over to the drawer where Joseph's black book was. Slowly she opened the drawer, hoping to see it there. It was gone. He'd taken it with him. The same sinking feeling she'd now grown accustomed to returned. She laid there awake all night long. She placed periodic calls to the hotel with no answer. Her mind started to gather all of the pieces together. He was having an affair or several affairs. She was sure of it! *I am not about to let him schmooze his way out this time!*

When the clock finally reached a reasonable time and she thought her mama was awake, she called to tell her everything. She told her the story about that night he didn't come home because Richard was drunk, the black book, now this dream, and the fact the black book is missing again.

"I can't do this, Mama. I love him too much to share him with anyone else. I can't live a lie."

Her mother tried to comfort her but really just came up with excuses for Joseph. Granny and Papa had already witnessed their daughter go through so much. They didn't want to see her go through another divorce. They loved my dad and didn't want to see this marriage end.

"Maybe it's just your hormones. After having a baby sometimes these things happen," Granny said.

"No! No! No!" said Mama. "Whose side are you on anyway? There's a part of me that has known for a long time," she continued. "I just talked myself out of it. I let my mind overrule what my heart and soul knew to be true. I don't want to see him. I don't want to talk to him. I want to come home!" she said.

"Okay Sophia! Just calm down. Let me talk to your father about this. Joseph isn't due back home for a while so y'all are all right there in your home for now. Just breathe, get yourself together. We'll talk again soon."

Not long after the call ended with her mother the phone rang again. *It's Joseph* she thought. She looked at the ringing phone trying to decide if she wanted to answer it or not. Finally she picked up.

Joseph was furious! "Sophia! Do you know this hotel just told me I'm no longer allowed to be a guest here because my wife called here every fifteen minutes, all night long?! What has gotten into you? You can't go on behaving like this!!"

"Well I'm sorry to cramp your style Mr. Gartman. If you'd been sleeping in your room instead of laying up with that woman I wouldn't have been calling all night long would I?"

He was quiet on the other end of the line. Her rant continued. "I know what you're doing! In case you've forgotten, I don't do secrets! I don't do little black books! I don't do cheating husbands either!" She slammed the receiver down and fell across the bed into a puddle of tears.

A few days passed with no phone calls from my dad or from her mother. She decided to toughen up and deal with things one day at a time. Papa James ended up telling Granny Doris their home wasn't big enough to house the three of us, and that Sophia needed to stay at her own home and work on saving her marriage.

"After all," he said, "what will people think? Divorced again! Two children from two different men. Dammit, Doris! She needs to get it together! She has a very secure life, a nice house, a new car, vacations, anything she wants!"

None of that seemed to matter to my mother as much as being loved exclusively. She wouldn't settle for less, not now, not ever! She said she decided to hire a private detective to see if her intuition was really spot on before proceeding. The man she hired cleverly called the hotels posing as my dad's tax accountant and requested phone call statements from each of the hotels where he traveled. Sure enough, the records contained phone calls to some of his old friends from the little black book.

Several months passed. The time rolled around for Dad to come home for another visit. She did her wifely duty by picking him up from the airport, but there was a cold chill in the air. My dad decided to break the ice on the way home.

"What can I do Sophia? How can I fix this? You know you're the only woman I love."

"Okay then," she said. "You can call each of those women in that book. Tell them you're happily married, and you won't ever be calling them again, and you'll do it in front of me!"

Dad was a little tipsy from the airline cocktails on the way home and joked, "Can I do it tomorrow?" He made himself laugh with that witty line, but he was the only one laughing. "No Sophia, I won't do that," he said. He regained his composure. "You're being ridiculous. You don't just forget all the people you have known throughout your life because you get married. There are parts of my life and parts of this job that you're just going to have to understand."

"I'll never understand, Joseph Gartman! I don't want a relationship like that! I can't sleep with you without thinking about another woman being in your arms. I don't work like that!"

He just sat there shaking his head in disbelief. He said, "I can't believe this is happening. You're going to leave me because of some upset stomachs and a damn dream!? You're nuts!!"

Needless to say, it wasn't a very pleasant few days at home this time. He did enjoy spending some time with me and Marilyn, but the chill between them remained throughout his time at home. Mom had been working hard to get her pre-baby figure back and felt she was looking better than ever. She could tell he longed to be close to her but knew there was no chance of that. As soon as he left town she secured a storage locker to hold our household furnishings and scheduled a meeting with an attorney to file for divorce. She was as stubborn as a mule when she made up her mind to do something. Nobody could stop her. She had him served with divorce papers while he was on the road. She asked for $300.00 a month in child support, the minimum allowed by the state. She asked for hospitalization insurance and college tuition for me. Receiving divorce papers while he was on the road infuriated him, but I believe their egos were in a battle now. He would "show her" by signing them quickly and returning them to the attorney. The divorce was final in thirty days.

Granny and Papa added another big bedroom on the side of their house to make room for us, and mom kept all of our household items in storage. By this time Marilyn was ten years old and I was three. Mom said anytime dad wanted to come to town to visit us she arranged for Marilyn and me to be with granny and Papa and she left. She said he came as often as he could which wasn't very often.

Mom started to realize how difficult it was going to be to have a home for us outside of her mother and father's house. She was happy for the relief living with them offered financially. Silently she longed for dates, friends, and a life without her parent's rules. With this in mind she reached out to a lawyer in St. Petersburg, Florida where dad was living. He agreed to represent her for an increase in child support and take his fees from her court award. She knew my dad was living high on the hog in the big leagues, and she wanted her due.

CHAPTER 8

St. Pete

My mother walked into the St. Petersburg court-house for the child-support hearing feeling extremely nervous. She was so unsure of just exactly how it was going to feel to see him again. My dad Joseph was still just as handsome and alluring as ever. Completely charismatic, he could, and did, own a room from the moment he walked in. He had the kind of confidence and appeal that women crave.

Mom said she was worried about the judgment she knew he would be sending her way in regard to the added pounds she'd put on since the last time they'd seen one another. He never minced words during their marriage if she gained any amount of weight at all. As they both entered the courtroom others there waiting could feel the unnerving chemistry along with the "I'll show you" exchange of energy happening between them.

The attendant called "ALL RISE" as the judge entered the room. The judge was a beautiful ebony skinned lady with her hair pulled back neatly in a bun. She had high cheekbones and perfect make-up. She was truly the most attractive judge my mother had ever seen. They were first on the docket. They approached the podium in front of the smiling lady that mom said she felt was sitting so high on a throne. This judge was about to pass a judgment that would forever change all of our lives. The judge listened to the request for an increase in child support and without any hesitation slammed the gavel. She called for a decrease in child support from $300.00 a month to $225.00 and told my mother to get a job!

With that the judge gave a sneaky wink to my dad, and it was then mom said that she knew. This was not the first encounter for my father and the beautiful judge. She was sure they'd met one another before. She said my dad turned to give her an "I WIN" smile that became a look of sadness as she turned around for one more moment of eye contact with him before walking out of the courtroom as quickly as she could. She fought to hold back the tears until she reached her car where she let it all out while making the five hour drive back to Savannah to her mama, me, my sister Marilyn, and Silk Hope. Her mind and heart raced with questions of how this was even possible. Her heart was broken.

How could he?! I bet he slept with her. That smooth talkin' devil! I bet he paid her off! They were all suitable answers to her racing thoughts. *What am I going to do now?* Sobbing, she continued: *How will we live? Where will I work to support the three of us? How could I have been so foolish to fall for him?* She cried and beat on the dash of the large Pontiac when those feelings got so strong she just had to hit something. That car sure took a beating, just as she felt she had.

Pulling into the large, circular, sandy driveway lined with large, old, magnolia trees and blooming wisteria vines that hung like huge clumps of grapes, she'd finally made it home. The smell of marsh mud at low tide wasn't pleasant to newcomers, but it soothed my mother's soul. Granny Doris rushed out to meet her as soon as she saw the car pull in. She was smiling and gently clapping her hands in anticipation of good news until she saw Mom's face. There were make-up-less lines down both cheeks where the salty tears had ruined the facade of the overly confident woman left behind in St. Petersburg. She collapsed into her mother's arms and again began to sob as she told her the unbelievable story of the courtroom experience with Joseph. Her mother stroked her hair, rubbing both hands down her back, and said the words she longed to hear. "Don't worry now. We'll figure something out. Come on inside, get yourself cleaned up, and have something to eat. The girls will be home soon. We don't want them to see you like this."

Mom and Dad let enough time pass to heal some of the bitterness. They spoke to each other occasionally.

Jovial exchanges remained a common theme between them. She loved telling of how sometimes he would call her in the middle of the night after having been out drinking with the guys. She would say something like "What's wrong Joseph? Were all of the other numbers busy?" He would laugh and say, "You're still Number One baby. You're still number one." They did make a deal with one another that if either of them ever decided to remarry they would spend one more night together before making a lifelong commitment to another.

As I got to be a little older mom said she would occasionally drive me down to dad's home in St. Pete. She would confess that being around him was way too tempting for her. She felt that the chemistry and attraction they felt for one another in the beginning never really went away. She knew herself well enough to know she would go crazy trying to force any part of his baseball lifestyle to work for either of them. She started letting Marilyn fly down to St. Petersburg with me until I turned eight years old. By then she felt I was old enough to fly alone. There would always be a stewardess to make sure I made it to the connecting flight at the Atlanta airport. I would get the drill from mom before I left for Florida on the airplane. Remember your manners, make sure your fingernails stay clean, chew with your mouth closed don't fart in front of anyone, or pick your nose, and remember to pick up after yourself. When your father asks about me tell him I spend a lot of time in my leopard bikini at the beach.

I remember feeling like a robot. Trying to remember how I was supposed to behave, look, and act. Then when I got back home to mom, she would tell me to stop behaving so high and mighty. It was quite confusing for me, to say the least. Later in my young adolescent years when I flew down to visit my dad it was only once a year, not really sufficient time to build any kind of relationship. He would say things like "doesn't look like you've missed any meals" as soon as I got off the plane. I was hearing that if you want love and approval from your father you should not be overweight. That could be added to the list of things mom had already instilled ... manners, cleanliness ... perfection, I suppose. It was yet another downloaded belief pattern set in place.

After the child support hearing mom decided to sign up for school at a Savannah vocational school. She asked the school administrator which field of study would earn the most money for her and decided to study Industrial Maintenance. She went to school all day and worked for UPS from 5-9 p.m. after her school day washing and gassing up the trucks for the next day delivery drivers. Her school instructor took her class on a trip to visit the Savannah sugar refinery, Hercules, and Gulfstream. She wasn't at all interested in working on the repetitive mass-production lines. She decided to interview for a job in the lab at Hercules. She was hired on the spot. She worked at the chemical plant in the lab for nearly five years. I loved it when she brought little aluminum cups of hardened resin that she had written some sort of sweet message in for me before it solidified.

The job there allowed us to move out of granny and Papa's house. She had to work shift work, changing from seven to three, three to eleven, and eleven to seven. Marilyn would be responsible for getting me up for school when mom worked the seven to three shift, but it was an impossible task for her. I would cry all the way while she was trying to walk or sometimes drag me to school. I cried until my nose bled. I can't remember what it was about that school that I didn't like. It was enough of something for me to throw one heck of a fit not to go. Worn out from the entire fiasco, Marilyn would turn around, head back to the house, and we would both miss that day of school. Granny Doris would come to help when mom worked three to eleven or eleven to seven. It wasn't the easiest way of life. A cycle began. Mom would find a home for us to live in. Struggles with bills, motherhood, and work would wear her out, and then we would have to move back in with Granny and Papa.

There was one time we didn't go back to granny and Papas. We went to a motel on Hwy 17 where mom knew the manager. We'd been living in a nice house in a neighborhood called The Village just off of Abercorn Street in Savannah. I have lots of memories from that house. We had a privacy fenced back yard that backed up to the woods. We put raw eggs out on the back patio for the raccoons to find late in the afternoons. They were so cute to watch. They would tap a little hole in the top of the egg and turn it up like a baby bottle to drink the raw egg. In the summertime when we had a hard rain without lightning mom would say "Let's go play in the rain!" So we stripped down and headed out the sliding glass door to run free, laughing all the while. We ran and played in the cool summer rain. It was wonderful. Each of us had our own bedroom in that house. Marilyn's room was decorated with a green and yellow bedspread with matching curtains. Then there was my room, and next door to that was mom's bedroom. I'm quite sure I wasn't as excited as Marilyn about having my own room. Up until this house I'd always slept with my mom. Sleeping in my own bed, I felt alone and afraid. The fear really got trumped-up a notch one night when I awoke terrified at the sound of what I thought was my mother being brutally murdered in the room next to me. I sat straight up in my bed and began to cry, frightened to death. Mom came running into my room to comfort me, but she was naked and covered in sweat!

"Are you okay?" I asked her through my tears. She laughed and said, "Yes, I'm fine. Don and I were just wrestling."

She told me not to be afraid and to go back to sleep, but sleep never came. I may have been young, but I wasn't stupid. Just a few weeks earlier I had asked her where babies came from. She had my sister and her girlfriend Pam sit in the car with me at the Oglethorpe Mall while she went into the bookstore. She came out and handed me two books. The first one starred two

Ziggy-like cartoon characters; one a man and the other a woman. It talked about how the husband and wife loved to do things together. It showed them taking a shower together, their different body parts in a full cartoon, and explained how they loved each other so much they wanted to get as close as they could. That picture had the overweight Ziggy on top of his bride with no clothes on. The second book was all about animals. It showed chickens mating, and the next page showed the baby chicks. It showed dogs mating, and the next page had the baby puppies. Cats, kittens, and so on. I believe because her mother never educated her about anything she was always concerned that we learn correctly along with the correct anatomical name for each of our body parts. Unable to pronounce "vagina" as a young child, I called mine "my china." So it didn't take me long to figure out that Mr. Don Juan was in there breaking my mother's china! I got angry, and the next day I packed my suitcase and told my mom I was running away. I didn't like Mr. Don Juan. He only laid around on our couch reading books all day. She made light of my announcement and asked questions about where I might be heading with my packed bags.

My sister Marilyn was also angry. She went to Granny Doris and told her that our mom had Mr. Don Juan in the house several nights. She told granny how disgusted she was about the whole thing and asked if she could move back in with her and Papa. Our Granny Doris took it upon herself to call my father, Joseph. She told him that our mom had a man shacked up with us at our house. So my dad called her asking, "What in the world is going on Sophia?"

"Well, Joseph," she said, "it's been five years, don't you think it's time I had another man in my house?" He said, "Please tell your mother not to call me again." While she had him on the phone she asked him to please send me to private school as well. There had been many epidemics of head lice in the public school systems. My long, thick, curly hair had to be treated and gone through with a fine-tooth comb strand by strand to remove the nits. It was expensive, costly, and took days to complete. He agreed to send me to the private school.

I had to be tested for what seemed like days, but was actually only four hours for entry into Savannah Christian school. I remember being tired of being there for so long so I started filling in the bubbles on the answer key without any consideration of the questions. The results came back that I needed to repeat the second grade. Mom thought it wasn't a bad trade for me to repeat a grade for the opportunity to be in a private school. She didn't make me go to school. I could tell her that I missed her and wanted to stay home. Or I had a tummy ache or didn't feel well. She let me stay home. She let me miss so much time I was kicked out of Savannah Christian that same year.

She took a tumble down some slippery stairs at Hercules and hurt her tailbone. She was out of work under a workman's comp claim for a while. Not long after, the doctor released her to return to work but she was fired from Hercules. She said they told her she missed too much time from work because of her children. She always believed it was because she had sustained an injury, and they wanted to limit their liability. She filed a grievance with the union but got nowhere. She put all of our things into storage again. She and I went to the motel on Hwy 17 where she knew the manager, and he agreed to let us stay there free of charge for a while. She and Granny Doris were still not talking because of the whole Don Juan deal and Marilyn was still living with them.

Marilyn came to visit us at the motel. We were all piled up in the big king-sized bed watching the Walton's on T.V. During a commercial, mom turned to me and asked if I wanted to go live with my father down in Florida. She'd glorified him with stories of his glamorous lifestyle. Yes! Of course I wanted to go live the big life. Riding on airplanes every few days, being on television.

"Yes, I do want to go," I said. Then she raised her voice, demanding I get up right then and put all of my clothes in a paper bag. Obviously distraught, she said, "I'll make sure you go!" She ran into the bathroom and slammed the door behind her, locking it. She cried and wailed like she was dying. I remember crying too. I felt bad that my honesty was hurting her. She wouldn't unlock the door to let me in. I was careful after that to never talk about leaving her ever again. I remember feeling so guilty. Her happiness or right then, her unhappiness, somehow felt like my responsibility.

Marilyn got so mad with mom after that episode she called the car dealership and told them our mother had been fired and was planning to leave town with the Volkswagen bug she bought on credit. They came to the motel and repossessed the car. Mom had no choice but to make up with Granny Doris, and we moved back in with them on Salt Creek Road.

I loved living with Granny and Papa in Silk Hope. They sold some of the 11-acre parcel of land they had to a nice family who would be our neighbors, Kaye and Pete Bibbs. They had a lot of children. The oldest girl went to school with Marilyn and they were friends. The youngest boy was my age so we were close friends too. We called their mother Aunt Kaye, and I loved playing at her house. She babysat a lot of neighborhood children, and her husband worked at a big local dairy. She also made wedding cakes for extra income, and her house always smelled like buttercream icing. The counters were covered with beautiful roses she crafted to cover the cakes. Something inside each of us kids told us we better not touch the delicate-looking colorful flowers, and we never did. They cut a lot of corners to allow Aunt Kaye to be a stay-at-home mom with such a large family. They raised chickens for eggs and meat. I'll never forget watching with amazement Aunt Kaye grabbing hold of those chickens and giving them a quick spin around in a circle with a flip and twist of her wrist. She would then let loose of that chicken, and it ran around the yard for a while with a flopping head until it eventually fell over dead. There was a big pot of hot boiling water that she stuck the bird into headfirst holding it by the feet. That loosened the feathers so they could be plucked out easily. I still remember the wet feather smell. It's a one-of-a-kind smell, not easily forgotten. After that, the chicken was dressed and put into the freezer. It was a huge operation the whole family took part in, but they did so many chickens it only had to be done a few times a year. They also raised rabbits for food, and I watched that process too. After tasting it at her dinner table once, I decided that was enough, even though it does "taste like chicken," as they say. Rabbits were far too cute for me to think about eating any more of them. I played over there every afternoon and on the weekends until the sun went down. Granny would put a long broomstick out on the porch with a red cloth hung on it like a flag. That was the signal that it was time for me to come home or that dinner was ready.

I would have preferred to stay there at the Bibbs' house. I loved the way their family was. They never seemed to bicker and argue. They didn't have to move a lot. We all sat together at her big dining table to eat. She made pancakes so big they covered the whole plate. Sometimes we all sat on her front porch and took turns shaking the Mason jar, turning the cream Mr. Pete brought home from the dairy into homemade butter. She treated me like one of her own, even making me stand with my nose in the corner when I had done something wrong. Like when Michael and I got caught playing doctor or show-and-tell. I remember he was my first kiss. I was in the second grade. We were sitting on the crosstie steps along the side of their home. I got mad at him because he didn't kiss me like I'd seen women get kissed on the soap operas my mother watched. We played outside all day long, finding sticks that we pretended were guns, playing war. Each of us was hiding somewhere out of sight. When you spotted one of the other players, you had to make a loud shooting noise with your voice "pee ouh" and announce to your victim that "you got him." Hide-and-go seek, Dodgeball, Mother May I, and Red Rover, these were some but not all of the games we played outside. She had a giant swing set in the backyard too. It was considered punishment for us to be kept inside for any reason. Outside was freedom, imagination, and fun.

Granny and Papa's house held many fond memories too. I learned to ride my bike on the hard, sandy, circular drive. I remember the first time I kept it level enough not to turn over. It was a true feeling of independence as I felt the breeze on my face I pedaled faster. I made many mud pies there in that front yard too, confiscating granny's kitchen utensils to dig in the dirt. Sometimes I got brave enough to grab an egg or two from her fridge to make my mud pies a little more moist.

My Papa could always be found in one of two places if he was home. In his chair inside the house in the living room listening to Paul Harvey on his radio. That's where I learned the words to the song *Delta*

Dawn. When he wasn't there he could be found outside the side door just off of the dining room. Down the cement stairs to the right was his old barber chair. The ground at the base of the chair was covered in large leaf English Ivy. It was a perfect place for him to hide his pint of whiskey where granny couldn't find it. It was there in that chair he told me if I wanted to go fishing with him I would need to learn how to rig a line and bait my own hook. He would take me fishing, but he told me he had no interest in doing everything for me once we got to the fishing hole. I agreed to learn how to do all of it with great excitement. First to tie the hook onto the line making nine passes around before putting it through the loop. Then you pulled the knot down tight. Next, you anchored that split-shot sinker to the line with a bite to close it with your back teeth. I recommend using pliers to do this, but that's not how Papa taught it. That sinker goes about two inches above the hook. Last was to decide how deep you needed to fish and put the bobber on the line at that depth. It was a simple freshwater rig. Then I learned to cast the line from the reel right there in the yard. When I got good he kept his promise and took me fishing. Once there, he taught me how to take my own fish off the hook and how to clean them when we got home.

Inside granny would teach me things like how to braid. She tied three pieces of the thick yarn to one of her bedposts. Then she showed me how to interweave them to create a braid. She also tried to teach me how to crochet, but I had absolutely no interest in that, or in learning to sew on her Singer sewing machine. I did love to look at her World Book Encyclopedias though. Especially the one with the human body. There were transparent pages that layered each body system on top of the other. You could see just the bones, then add the muscles, then the nerves, veins, and arteries, and finally the skin. I was fascinated. I must have spent hours studying those pages and flipping them back and forth. The encyclopedia with the frog in it had the same kind of anatomy pages. My favorite toy back then was a plastic pretend medical bag. Inside were a stethoscope, a syringe to give a shot, and a hammer to test reflexes. I loved listening to the heartbeats of our family members and administered shots when they didn't feel well. I would say even at that young age that when I grew up I would be a doctor.

I thought my sister Marilyn was the most beautiful woman alive. She was seven years older than I. I wanted to be just like her, and I wanted to be around her and her friends all of the time. I was a pain in the ass though. Mom would make her take me everywhere she went. I always came up with something to tattle on her for. She was speeding, or she smoked a cigarette, it didn't matter what it was. I was a tattletale. I guess it was my way of getting her attention. I used to pick on her constantly. If she was talking to a boy on the phone, I would lift the other receiver in the house and lay it down. Then I would run and hide. She thought I was listening to her conversation. She would have to ask whoever she was talking to- to hold on while she hung up the other receiver. As soon as she went back to her phone call I would emerge from my hiding place and do it again. She would call out, not knowing where I was hiding and threaten to kill me. I can't believe she never did, but I do know she thought about it a lot.

CHAPTER 9

Tybee

After getting fired from Hercules mom took several different jobs as a bartender in some of the local watering holes. Her quick wit and sense of humor made it possible to earn more tip money than she could have made working a minimum-wage job anywhere. She took a summer job as a nanny for some record producers who lived in a beautiful oceanfront home at the end of 14th street on Tybee Island. Mom and I lived downstairs. There was an entrance and one bedroom with a full bath down there.

Marilyn who was now fifteen years old had grown tired of the constant moves. She didn't like our gypsy style of life anymore. She also felt overly responsible for me, her little sister. She felt like a surrogate mother. So she moved in with some older friends who also lived near Silk Hope, Patsy and Troy Fordham. Their family had known mom's family from the time they moved to Silk Hope. They would provide some stability, security, safety, and love for Marilyn. She grew into the most beautiful young lady. She quickly drew the attention of local photographers and small-town publications that put her bathing-suit photos on the cover and as the centerfolds of the *Georgia Fishing World* magazine with great regularity. She won Ms. Coppertone on the beach in front of the house where mom was the nanny that summer. People thought she and mom were sisters. Mom always got a thrill out of that! They got along much better not living together. That nanny job lasted one summer. They wanted mom to stay full-time and clean the house while their children were in school. Being the housemaid was not in the trunk of my mom's talents. She declined to take the position. The couple partied like rock stars anyway. Mom would often end up watching the children on her days off because the parents couldn't get out of bed from an all-nighter the night before.

I was given a lot of freedom to roam the island as a child. I made friends with Mario, a Greek man who had a little restaurant on 16th street. He let me wait tables in the summertime for tip money plus one Gyro a day. I spent the tip money at the local arcade on the corner playing Ms. Pacman at the Tybee Island amusement park, or at the oceanside water slide that was over 200 steps to the top!

Mario had beach bathing suit modeling shots like those in *Sports Illustrated* of my sister Marilyn framed and hanging on the walls of his small restaurant. Mom said a movie producer who was in town filming came into Mario's restaurant to eat and saw the photographs. He asked Mario how to find the young lady in the photos. He gave the guy our mother's contact information. Mom told the producer that Marilyn was out of town on a trip with her boyfriend's family, so the guy asked that she please get in touch with him when she returned. He gave her his business card. Mom said he wanted her to fly out to where he was. She said she told Marilyn about it and gave her the man's card, but Marilyn's boyfriend didn't want her to call him, so she never did. I often wonder how different her life may have been if she had.

I also made friends with Robert Flip who owned the airbrush shop where he created unique T-shirts and car tags for vacationers. He would let me hang paper towels on the wooden spray boards and practice painting bubble letters and palm trees with the airbrush. I knew I could always go to Capt'n Christopher's restaurant and bar to have a burger, fries, and a Coke. I got whatever I wanted and charged it to mom's bar tab. I was very mature, independent, and very street smart to be so young. The one thing I did fear was being left alone at home after dark.

Mom would frequent the local bars sometimes in the early evening or on her days off. I would beg her not to go. She would say. "You know I'm more than your mommy. I'm also a person who needs friends and a little fun once in a while."

Mom always assured me that the record producer couple she worked for and their two children were just up the stairs if I needed anything. I never bothered them but would cry myself to sleep waiting for her to return. After that job ended we moved around a bit more. There were at least three more Tybee houses we lived in and one efficiency motel. Always back- and -forth from there to Granny and Papa, and then off to the next place she found. The cycle continued for years.

My mother was tending bar at a Tybee lounge when she heard the television announcer congratulate the umpire, Joseph Gartman, on his recent marriage. The owner of the bar said mom turned white as a ghost. They had both remained single for nine years. Mom had taken a few lovers to comfort her through the years, but nothing that ever got serious enough for the consideration of marriage. Joseph hadn't kept his end of the deal they made with one another to share one more night together before they committed to another in marriage. She was devastated. I suppose her nine-year separation from him felt finalized in a way that it hadn't before he decided to re-marry. She would later confide that she always held the fantasy that after he got all of that womanizing out of his system he would be back, and they would be together again.

We were living in a small house at Tybee when she told me she said a prayer and asked God to send her another man to love. She was tired of being alone. The very next day a man knocked on the door asking if this was her poodle. Joe-Joe was our silver mini-toy poodle who had wandered off when she let him outside. Mom says she was quick to assume this was the man God had sent in response to her prayer.

Sometime later she did marry him but would joke that he was really the devil in disguise. Kenny was as good as gold when he was sober, but became a strange, violent man when he drank. If the two of them went out drinking together it was as if the gates of hell flung open. Some of the fights they got into usually ended in physical damage to one or both of them, or some part of our property being destroyed. It was quite frightening at times. I called 911 on more than one occasion, but the one I remember most was when he chased her through the motel with a pistol. Regardless, she stayed with him. The volatile nature of the relationship kept us on the move from house to house, town to town. Always looking for a place to start over after a blowout.

One such move was to the small country town of Guyton, Georgia. I believe they thought if they moved away from the party atmosphere at the beach to a more wholesome place things would be different. That was 1982, which turned out to be one heck of a year. Papa James had an aneurysm and died on the operating table while they were trying to fix it.

Mom couldn't make herself go to the funeral. She was completely overcome with grief, feeling as though she'd lost the "best man" ever in her life. She asked my Granny Doris to please bring her a lock of his hair.

Granny forgot about it until the last minute when the casket was graveside. So afraid of disappointing her daughter, she asked the attendants to re-open the casket so she could fulfill Sophia's request for a lock of her father's hair.

This infuriated both Peggy and Roger. They thought the whole of it obscene and unacceptable. Mom said it pretty much ended the relationship between her and Peggy. Funny thing is, as awful as the relationship had become, mom never tried to prevent me or Marilyn from having a relationship with our Aunt Peggy or her children, our cousins. We were all close, and Aunt Peggy never talked bad about mom in front of us. She always threw a huge Christmas Eve party where all of our family drew names to exchange gifts. My cousin Louise and I were the babies in both our families. We would sneak the spiked punch and walk around the neighborhood with friends singing Christmas carols. I even lived with Aunt Peggy for a while when I was in elementary school. I can't remember the exact hardship my mom was having that time. I liked living there though. Louise and I were close. We scratched each other's backs each night until we fell asleep. We sang songs from the radio and recorded funny skits on her cassette recorder. Then we would listen to the cassette and laugh at all of the funny ad-lib stuff we came up with. Aunt Peggy's house had some structure. We got up at a certain time, had breakfast together, made our beds, got dressed, packed our lunches. There was a system of order in her house. It felt good.

I don't think my mom and her brother Roger ever spoke again after Papa's funeral. Roger divorced his first wife Judith after they had three children. I don't recall mom saying the year that happened, but all three of the kids were young. He remarried to a lady named Bethany. The story has it, according to mom, that Granny Doris went out to visit them once. Bethany's diamond bracelet disappeared after Granny's visit, and she was questioned about it. Mom said Granny Doris was devastated by the accusation, and constantly cried and complained to her about why her boy never came to visit.

"He would send a plant or flowers on Mother's Day," she said, "But he rarely ever came to see his mother again." Mom became vengeful toward her brother Roger on her mother's behalf. She was angry that he seemed controlled by his new wife, so she chose not to see or talk to her brother again for that reason. Mom was good at sticking to her guns when she wrote someone off in her life. When she was done, she was done. We did go visit his first wife, our Aunt Judith, and all three of her children, our first cousins.

I was only twelve when Papa died, and it was my first experience with death. I remember getting so angry and blaming the doctors for it. Then I cried more tears than I had ever cried. It's hard to come to terms with someone being there one moment and gone the next. I remember thinking he looked like one of those people at the wax museum when I saw and touched him at the funeral home. It was quite obvious to me that a part of him was not there anymore. The part that made him my Papa was gone.

My stepfather Kenny tried to make the sorrow-filled time better for me and mom. He made some stilts out of some leftover wood he had lying around and showed me how to walk on them around the yard. He taught me how to drive his old work truck down the dirt road in front of the old farmhouse where we lived. All of the gears were on the steering column. Three on the tree, they called it. I scared the shit out of both of us trying to navigate the clutch, and the gas, all the while keeping us between the ditches on the slippery clay dirt road. I was still three years away from even having a learner's permit but living in the country you got away with a lot more than those city kids did. I got good enough at driving that old truck that they would let me drive to my best friend Hanna's house. She lived on a farm about a half-mile down the road. I would help her and her two brothers do their chores so we could play. It was a great place to live until mom and Kenny had another big blow-out. He went to jail, and mom asked Hanna's parents if I could live with them for a while until she got things straightened out. It wasn't strange to move at least once a year. I always begged her not to take him back. He would cry and promise to change, and she would believe him. I never did.

I have a friend who describes her childhood as a bipolar upbringing. She says, "It was either a whole lot of fun or scary as hell! Never a lot of in-between those two extremes." I felt this was the perfect analogy for my childhood years too.

By this time mom was having repetitive back surgeries to repair cascading disc damage that seemed to have started with the fall she had at Hercules. She now lived in a great deal of pain every day, took an array of prescriptions, and slept a lot. Her working days were over, and she felt doomed to be totally dependent on Kenny for our survival. We moved to Augusta, Georgia for a construction opportunity for him, but that was short-lived because he got drunk and piled all of our belongings up in a pile and set them on fire! The flame got so huge someone called the fire department. We caught a bus back home to live with Granny Doris again. Kenny was begging his way back into our lives, claiming he found religion. She believed him again, so we moved out to Midway, Georgia together. He was reading the Bible every day and wanted to pray with her a lot. All of that changed when she found his pot growing spot in the woods beside our house. She sent me to Savannah to stay with my sister Marilyn while she called the law on Kenny. She said she wanted him to get into trouble for it so he would learn a lesson.

While I was at Marilyn's I called my father. I told him everything that was going on. He asked if I wanted to come down to Florida and live with him and his wife Carol. They were living near the beach. I could go to school and have a stable life without all of the chaos I had grown so accustomed to in Georgia. I said "Yes!" He arranged my flights, and my sister took me to the airport. I was excited to start a new life there. I was so hopeful about living in one place, making long-term friends, nobody fighting or going to jail. They took me shopping for clothes and enrolled me in school. I loved that when we went to the grocery store Carol bought whatever she wanted. I was so accustomed to having to add as we went down each aisle and shopping creatively to make the most of the small food budget my mom had. I remember thinking I was going to be just like that one day, able to purchase what I wanted without having to look at the price tag.

Carol was a beautiful lady. Her hair and make-up looked perfect all the time, even when she woke up in the mornings. She was tall and curvy with dark auburn hair, olive skin, and brown eyes. She had big boobs and hips with a tiny little waist. She had lots of cool clothes and jewelry. I loved her sports car. She named it "Megan." It was a 280 ZX turbo. Megan talked to us in the sexiest sultry voice. "Your lights are on," she would say. Carol liked to have fun, just like my mom did. The two of them actually had a lot in common. Both of them are kinda tomboyish and gorgeous all wrapped up in one. Carol knew how to ride motorcycles and how to pilot a small plane. She danced around the house cleaning to Neil Diamond songs on the radio. She also loved to cook good, interesting recipes, just like my mom did.

Carol had done some things to try to bond with me after she and my dad married. She took me to Circus World where we had our faces painted like clowns. We visited her mom in Orlando where we all went skinny dipping in her backyard pool after the sun went down. She was different but easy to talk to. Like a friend.

Everything was going great living with them until I talked to my mother on the phone. She cried and pleaded with me to come back home. I didn't want to. I really liked being there, so I decided I wouldn't talk to her anymore. It was too painful.

One day, in the middle of class at school, I got called to come to the office for a phone call. It was her, crying hysterically. She was telling me how awful life was for her without me. She started making promises to get me things if I came home. A horse, a moped, whatever I wanted. It was killing me to hear her so upset like that. I felt I could save her all of the anguish by returning. That day after school I told my father I wanted to go back to Georgia. He was angry I could tell, and Carol was upset too. I learned that he had already dropped a bundle to his lawyer in the fight against my mother for my permanent custody. I imagine he probably had a good case. After all, there were police records of the fights, the fire in Augusta, and the pot growing expedition in Midway. Surely that was enough to prove an unfit life for a child. Dad and Carol were careful, and they never discussed any of the legal proceedings in front of me. I totally admire both of them for that now. I hadn't fear or worry in the time I spent with them until those calls from my mother came in. My father said he didn't want me there if I didn't want to be there, and he arranged my flights back to Georgia. He didn't understand that I didn't want to be in Georgia, I wanted to stay right there with them, but I felt responsible for her happiness, or unhappiness, just like that time in the motel! She was in pain and I had the power to fix it, by going home. Hindsight? I would've been better served by a good therapist, rather than a plane ticket back home, but I guess that wasn't the plan.

Mom kept the promises she made, and they bought a horse we named Shamrock because she was born on St. Patrick's Day. She was a beautiful horse, but I couldn't ride her. Each time I tried she laid down like she was gonna roll. It scared the smack out of me, so I jumped off. She also got the moped for me which I absolutely loved to ride, until Valentines' Day in 1984 when I pedaled to start it and pulled out of the store parking lot in front of a car! I flew up on top of the hood and bounced back off of it onto the ground in front of her car. I tried to get up as fast as I could but quickly realized I couldn't! Strangers were stopping to cover me with their coats and jackets. It didn't take long for my mother to show up. She had an eerie sixth sense that told her anytime something happened to one of us. Years before, Marilyn had a dirt-bike accident with one of her friends, and mom knew it the moment it happened. It was like she had a direct line to each of us that warned her when something bad happened. It freaked us out on more than one occasion growing up.

The ambulance never showed up so she and Kenny took me to the hospital. All of the soft tissue and muscle in my upper right thigh was crushed, along with any opportunity to ever professionally model. I was only 14 years old, and already 5 feet, 11 inches tall. I guess God had other plans for me. I was unable to walk without the worst cramps and spasms in the world. I was homeschooled for three months and ended up with a huge permanent dent in my right thigh. I didn't care if I EVER got on anything with only two wheels again! To me, my motorcycle days were over!! When I heard my mother was talking about a lawsuit I asked her not to sue anyone. It was a school classmate's mother who hit me. I'd already heard she was too shaken to drive again and that she may have been in therapy of some sort. My young teenage brain could not understand it would have been the insurance company getting sued, not my friend's mother specifically. Children should never know the undertakings of adults or the business things that need to be taken care of like that. It's too much for a young mind to worry about

CHAPTER 10

Wild Child

I moved out as soon as I was able to drive. Mom got a settlement from workman's comp on her last back injury, and she gave me a thousand dollars for a car. I went to Springfield Ford and told the man how much money I had and asked if he had anything I could buy. He showed me a white 1979 Ford Fairmont. It had a great sound system in it and it ran. That was all I really cared about. I decided I was too smart for school, so I dropped out. Besides, I'd been to thirteen different schools up to that point, often deciding to head to the beach rather than homeroom.

I was living with an older lady friend of mine for a while. My mother gave me the $225.00 a month child support checks my dad sent, so I shared it with my friend and her husband to cover my food expenses. I did attend a modeling school in Savannah and took small jobs where the indention in my upper thigh from that moped accident could be camouflaged. I worked as a model at a few jobs locally, at the Oglethorpe Mall in Savannah, and the new mall at Shelter Cove that opened on Hilton Head Island.

I got pregnant by my friend's little brother whom I had a fling with that summer. By all accounts, my life was taking the same path my mother's had. I was a week away from being eighteen years old when we married because it was the "right thing to do," so society said. It didn't last. We were no more than children ourselves. We divorced and our two-year-old daughter Crystal and I moved back home with my mother and stepfather Kenny. Once there I studied for my GED and returned to school, this time to be a nurse's assistant. I landed a home health job with a company on Wilmington Island and loved the work, but the pay wasn't enough to sustain us, so I started bartending. That's when I would meet who would become husband #2, Harvey. We had a lot of fun together. I worked as a bartender at a local country-western bar and dance club named Randall's that we frequented. In the summertime, I headed back to Tybee, bartending at the beach. I learned to play golf, and Harvey taught me how to shoot a mean game of pool. We were on Pool and Dart leagues and played both in local bars all over town. We enjoyed playing golf together too. My mom and Kenny were living about five miles from Harvey in Pooler, Georgia so they babysat Crystal most of the time for Harvey and me to play. And play we did. My life had been so slow and confined to the little country town of Clyo, Georgia where I lived with Crystal's daddy Seth. That Savannah nightlife felt like Las Vegas to me. I absolutely love to dance and couldn't get enough of it! I always felt Crystal's father was a homebody who didn't even like to cross the Effingham County line to go anywhere or do anything. I would sit in the swing in our yard listening to Reba McEntire sing the song lyric, "Is there life out there, so much she hasn't done." That was my song! Harvey was just the opposite. We stayed on the go and partied our asses off. I had received the Depo shot as birth control because I was horrible at remembering to take my birth control pills in a timely fashion. That's how my second daughter Amber came along. I never had another period after the shot. I went out for a home pregnancy test and guess what, again we did the "right thing" and married. Amber was born exactly five years and one day after Crystal.

Dad got chosen to call the World Series and flew Harvey and me to all of the games. That was a week-long party and one of the best weeks of my life. We ate and drank at the finest restaurants in both teams' cities, often closing them down. We slept most of the days away only to wake before game time to get dressed and do it all over again. Dad got a lady's version of the World Series ring for me. The gift was quite special because he'd sent me the man's ring, just like his from the first World Series he called, nearly twenty years earlier. I was only eight years old then and although my Granny Doris was supposed to have it put away in a safe place for me, somehow it disappeared. It took me four years to tell him it was gone, and I cried like a baby when I broke the news to him. They can't be remade, the mold is broken. As early as a few months ago I had the idea to search the internet for it, thinking if it had been stolen and sold, there may be a miraculous chance of me finding it on the World Wide Web. Teams' names were on either side and a huge diamond was on the top with my name engraved inside the gold band. It would be a miracle to have it back.

After baby girl Amber came, I was ready to settle down. I dreamed of a quiet life in the country where we could raise the girls together with our dog Rocky and be happy. I had had my fill of barrooms, bartending, and the "party-hard" life we both enjoyed throughout our dating. There was a constant inner whisper that seemed to say to me, "You want more out of this life, don't settle." Harvey hadn't expressed any interest in the changes I craved, and I didn't know how to make them on my own. I didn't have a decent way to support the three of us if I decided to leave. I went with Amber and Crystal to visit my father and his wife Carol in Florida. I told him how desperately I needed a career. He'd been trying to talk me into attending Massage Therapy school for years. He said he thought I would enjoy doing it and it would be lucrative. He received a lot of massages while traveling on the road, and he had a hunch it was going to turn into a big business. I listened to him talk but kinda blew it off. Just a few hours later I was thumbing through a local magazine in his kitchen and noticed an advertisement for a local massage school. The ad said to send off for a school catalog for more information. So I thought, *That won't hurt, I'll just see what it says.* I called the school to have one sent to my home with Harvey back in Georgia. I didn't even tell my father I did that. We finished up our visit, and I drove back home with both of the girls. A few days later the brochure for the school arrived. I remember feeling surprised as I looked through it, noticing how "medical" it was. Anatomy and Physiology, Massage history, and practice. The owner of the school was the therapist for the Florida Marlins. I was impressed and rather excited to jump in. I'd already aced my A&P class during my nursing assistant study at South College. The course was full-time, Monday-Thursday, eight hours a day for six months. I had never even had a massage. I called my father and told him I thought I wanted to take his advice and learn massage. I'd sent for a brochure for a school near him in Melbourne. I thought I could make arrangements for the girls here in Georgia while I stayed with him during the week and would come home to my family on the weekends.

It was by far the most **BOLD** decision I felt I'd ever made. Like my friend LaTrelle always said, "when you have **BOLD** there is always MAGIC that follows." The magic began. My dad agreed to pay for my school and give me expense money for gas and lunches if I was serious. So I called Crystal's father who was remarried to a nurse in Savannah and asked if our daughter Crystal could live with them and go to school. I would have her every weekend when I came home, or when Harvey drove down to Florida he could bring her. I asked my sister Marilyn if Amber could stay with her for the same kind of schedule. This left Harvey not being responsible for anyone other than himself. They both agreed. I couldn't believe I was about to leave my kids and husband four days a week to launch a new career. There were no massage schools close to my home though. The choices were Atlanta or Florida. At least in Florida I would have somewhere to live while I attended. The good news is there were not very many massage therapists in Savannah. Once back home I would be able to hang my own shingle.

The adjustments that had to be made while I was in school down there were not easy ones. I had always worked and had my own spending money. Now I had to ask for every dollar. I really wanted to get a little side gig somewhere so that I could have my personal freedom again. What if I wanted to go for wings and beer with everyone after school? I needed my own moolah. My dad refused. Our newly forming relationship with one another would be tested in the largest of ways.

I laid out of school one day when I was scheduled to take an Anatomy and Physiology test. I had been trying to reach Harvey back home all night with no luck and was sleep-deprived. I decided to stay home, study, and make up for the test the next day. I thought

I hid the fact that I stayed home from my dad, but somehow, he found out. He was furious! He came back to the pool house where I was living and told me to pack my shit and head back to Georgia. He said that I was just like my mother and would never finish a damn thing! I started crying and told him that wasn't true. I told him how I tried to call Harvey all night with no answer, which must have triggered some "not so pleasant memories" about my mother in him. He cut me to the quick, just like I had seen him do with some of those baseball players on television.

He let me know what it meant to "answer the bell," which meant no matter what has happened or is happening in your life the most important part is to "show up!" It doesn't matter if you are hung-over, didn't sleep, have diarrhea, lost a leg, whatever the reason, you always "SHOW UP!" He wasn't going to take my tearful pleas as an excuse! I was about to be ejected from the game! I had failed by not showing up at school, and he wasn't going to stand for it.

Then, something he said hit a nerve, and I got mad, too. More than anything in this world I hated being compared to my mother. Him telling me I was just like her lit a fire in my gut that still burns today! I told him I would not quit and go home! I would move out of his house and in with one of my classmates. I would get a job and pay my own way, but I would not quit!! I believe he knew exactly what he was doing, and I believe any other kind of response from me and he would have sent me packing.

My father's love was tough, but my soul would require that in this lifetime to grow. My mother let me do just about whatever I wanted. I needed to hear NO! I woke up the next morning and went to school. He never brought it up again. I would use the fire he created in me to power through and finish school just to prove to him that I "could" finish something. Really, after it was all said and done, I had proven this to myself although I didn't know it at the time. That decision, that act of pure will to persevere and not give up, would create a momentum of knowing I could accomplish anything that I wanted to for the rest of my life.

I also had to get used to sharing living space with my stepmom Carol while I was there for school. It was sometimes difficult. I grew up in a household where we shared everything, ate what we wanted to from the fridge, and came and went as we pleased. We borrowed clothes from one another's closets. I brought all of that with me to her home.

The "one for all and all for one" living concept was foreign to her. She had been an only child, and never had children. I believe the idea of someone coming into her home and acting as if it were their own repulsed her. I believe it still does. She taught me and is still teaching me about boundaries. We never really had a mother-daughter relationship. It was more like a friendship, and still is. She was my go-to for all of the years I viewed my dad as a hard-ass. I would talk to her about what I needed, and she was the bridge for our communication.

Massage school would prove to be the best thing I had ever decided to do. I clicked with it more than anything else I'd ever done or dreamed of doing. I was learning about so much more than the massage technique. I was learning a true mind, body, and spiritual healing. It's where I got my first dose of "spirituality." Yes, I'd visited several churches while I was growing up. I watched as others "got the spirit" at the Church of God. I felt the chills of a perfectly sung gospel song by the choir, and I cried right along with the sinners who went to the altar up in front of the congregation while the decision song was played. I myself had professed my own belief and love of Christ this way.

Massage school was different. It was as if I was learning to get in touch with the holiness that was within me - my own spirit, a part of me that had a voice of its own. One that only professed love and the oneness that connects us all. No matter the country, color, religion, or class. Gay or straight, rich or poor. In our most basic form we are one and the same. I learned how to love, nurture, and grow from that place of spirit, how to live, feel, and forgive.

More was impressed upon me in those six months of massage school than had ever been sitting on a church pew. I learned about energy healing and the power of meditation. I learned, and we practiced with classroom experiments, how our thoughts can be felt by others. I experienced this first-hand one day while we were trading massages in school. My dad was a stickler for cleanliness at home. While I was massaging my classmate I was thinking about all of the cleaning I had to do when I got home after school. I was going over all of it in my mind while I was working on her. I saw myself vacuuming, mopping, cleaning the glass doors, and so on.

The next day in school my classmate said "I don't know what got into me after that massage yesterday! I went home and cleaned my entire house!!"

Well I'll be damned, I thought, *it's true.* My thoughts of cleaning throughout her massage sent her home to clean! I'm ever so careful what I think when I'm massaging anyone. I try not to think at all. I say my prayers, asking to be used as a vessel of healing by all heavenly energies, and that coupled with the music and both of our energies makes a kind of "dance." It's a different dance with every person who comes in. I learned about the chakras, and how premature infants grow so much faster when massaged, and the healing powers of essential oils, and so much more.

I'd found my niche in life. I was changing, growing, and evolving quickly. This would be the beginning of a new life for me. Every cell in my body knew it. I graduated in 1997 but it wouldn't be the end of my learning. I became a sponge and continued to study with the great healers and teachers, through their books, seminars, and classes.

My first job as a therapist was at a hair salon named *The Wizard of Ahhhs* on Drayton Street in downtown Savannah. A lady named Renee owned the salon. We hit it off right away when she suggested we should walk next door to Pinky Masters lounge and talk about business over a White Russian. I rented her loft and started working there with her the following week and have never looked back. I would drive home in tears realizing that I could earn in a few hours what took me all weekend tending bar. I was, and still am, ever so grateful for the opportunity for this change in my life. I always remember to send a message to my dad and Carol thanking them around February 22 which is my graduation anniversary.

One year later I took a job at a high-end Aveda salon on Perry Street. It was just a few blocks from where I started at the *Wizard of Ahhhs.* The salon was very hip, chic, and trendy. The owner would feature different artist's work, often hosting openings for them. I was lucky enough to get one of Laura DiNello's prints. She has become quite famous.

While working there I was named "Best Massage Therapist in Savannah" by a poll put out by the Creative Loafing paper. A testimony, I felt, to my love of the healing art. I feel it was divinely ordered. Every person played a part. My dad suggested it over and over again until I answered the call. Carol agreed to let me come there to live. My sister Marilyn and Crystal's father helped with the children so I could take the opportunity. This along with my willingness to take a chance and be **bold**. This was "good stuff" and my childhood dreams of becoming a healer were being realized. Not as a doctor the way I dreamed way back then. This was better. Healing by considering all three levels of the person, mind, body, and spirit. This was a holistic approach. When there is a disturbance in one there is a disturbance in all. They are not independent of one another. Western medicine is starting to come around to this well-known theory, but there's a lot of "business" in our medical system.

It didn't take long for Harvey and me to separate after I came home and began my career as a therapist. He'd grown accustomed to the single lifestyle and the freedom he had while I was away at school. I hadn't been an angel either. The changes that had taken place within me made us more worlds apart than they'd been before I left for school. The owner of the massage school warned everyone in her opening speech that radical change was about to take place in all of our lives. She couldn't have been more right about that.

The change has continued to happen gradually throughout the years. More and more of what no longer serves the highest and best interest of the highest part of me has fallen away like the shucks on an ear of corn. I took the girls and moved back in with my mother and Kenny at the place they called Tarver Pond in Springfield, Georgia until I could save enough money for a home of my own.

My dad and his wife Carol came up to look for a house with me. He'd agreed to let me use his name for a mortgage to get a decent sized home in Springfield to raise the girls. For the first time in my life, I was able to provide for myself and my children. An indescribable feeling! They would have one place to call home.

Amber was five years old by this time and Crystal was ten. They would go to only a handful of schools. They could enjoy lifelong friendships, be allowed to play any sport they wanted to. They could be in the band or other school clubs, beauty contests, or go to proms, all of the things I missed out on. It was my first taste of true independence. My mom was only about seven miles away, so she could help me with the girls after school. With good schools and a positive sports and family dynamic, Effingham County was, and still is, a great place to raise children.

CHAPTER 11

Silk Hope

Tarver Pond was a five-acre beautiful piece of land mom and Kenny decided to purchase and settle down on after sixteen years of marriage. Kenny built a playhouse with a front porch overlooking the pond for the girls to play in and a Tom Sawyer raft for them to pole around the pond. Kenny was quite a talented craftsman. He could build anything. They had geese and pet goats. It really was a mini farm. The children just loved it. Mom planted all manner of bushes, herbs, flowers, and more. She loved to write and said she was trying to create a peaceful environment so that she could finish all of the books she'd started over the years. With her constant worry about Kenny coming home drunk and tearing something up, coupled with the worsening back pain, and a mysterious neurological neuropathy happening on the right side of her body, she never finished her manuscripts.

Kenny built a pole barn overlooking the pond to entertain and have cookouts. He built horse stables to house two of Marilyn's horses and the ponies they bought for the girls, Crystal and Amber.

Mom would occasionally start a beautiful painting but none of those ever got completed either. In fact, the scenery in her paintings over time began to look more gray, without foliage. The seasons appeared to be winter, and they felt lifeless, cold, empty, and void.

Early one Spring morning in 1998, the phone rang, and my mom answered. "Hello," a lady's voice on the other end of the line asked, "Are you Sophia?"

"Yes," mom replied. "Who is this?" she questioned. She seemed frustrated by the lady's intrusive questioning.

The lady continued, "Did you have a baby on March 25, 1965?"

"Yes," mom said.

"I believe I'm your daughter," said the lady on the other end of the line.

My mom began to holler as loud as her body would allow. It was a sound that didn't seem human Crystal recalled. The bellow caused Kenny to come running into the house. He couldn't make out her words but was sure something terrible must have happened to one of us children because all mom could say was, "My baby! My baby!" She continued to clench the phone receiver ever so tightly to her ear, unable to speak. Thirty-three years of wondering, praying, hoping. The release, the emotions, and healing that were taking place at that very moment were so strong my mother thought she was dying. I suppose a part of her was.

Kenny was finally able to discern who it was on the phone after several more minutes of anxiously listening to her every word. He called mom's doctor for some nerve pills so she would eventually be able to rest.

The two of them talked on the phone for hours. Alexandra was her name. Alexandra Devonshire. She lived in Dallas, Texas with her husband John and their three children, Bryan, Linda, and Tonja. Alexandra worked with special-needs children at one of the local schools near their home. Mom just couldn't believe her ears. It all seemed too good to be true. Alexandra continued by telling mom the story of how long she'd searched for her. She paid several people to try to find her. Now that her search had finally found us, Alexandra was able to put two and two together. She figured out it was Jacob Krasnoff being so clever by changing Sophia's last name to Lucas at the hospital in Jesup. It was the one thing that threw everyone off.

She told mom how she'd reached a point that she was tired. Tired of coming up empty, tired of being disappointed, putting her own family on emotional roller-coaster rides as she searched, and paid all of these different people to search. Then one day one of the teachers she worked with came to school elated. This teacher was adopted too and told Alexandra she was able to find her own birth parents in Richmond Hill, Georgia, and they were planning a reunion.

This teacher asked Alexandra to put her information on the registries too. "Oh no," Alexandra told her. "I have given up on that," she said. She proceeded to tell her about the ups and downs of searching for her birth mother up to that point. Her teacher friend continued to persuade her to give it a go saying, "C'mon, it doesn't cost a dime. What do you have to lose?" She thought for a bit and wondered if she could put herself or her family through it again.

Alexandra had found much comfort through the years in her connection to God and her spiritual friends. So she prayed and poured her heart out to God, all of her fears, concerns, hopes, dreams. She laid it all out there on his altar. The next day at school she told the teacher she would love to give it a try.

"One last try," she said. "It's in God's hands now. Whatever the outcome, I'll accept it." She said that from August to March she filled out registries online after teaching her class, never hearing a word from anything or anyone. It had been eight months of diligence. Eight months of hoping, dreaming, imagining what it might be like to finally find her mother and not one peep.

One can only imagine how frustrated and defeated she must've been feeling. So Alexandra said she had one final talk with God about it. She told God if she was ever going to know her birth mother, he was going to have to be the one to find her. And that was it. She completely surrendered the search and said she actually felt relieved. It felt good to lay it down. She was tired. That's when it happened. That's when she received the one and only email. It truly was a miracle. A lady saw her entry on the registry and said in an email to Alexandra that she had access to records others did not. She thought she could help her. It was her hobby. She didn't charge at all for her services. She just appeared like an online angel. Sure enough, she was able to find our mom for Alexandra when no one else could!

The online angel gave her two phone numbers. One was Uncle Roger, and the other one was Aunt Peggy. She called Aunt Peggy first and explained who she was and that she was trying to find Sophia, her birth mother. Alexandra said Peggy gave her a whole host of reasons why she should never contact Sophia. One of the things she told her was that Sophia was a hopeless alcoholic.

It didn't work. Alexandra told Peggy she didn't care what kind of condition her mother was in. She had been searching for her whole adult life and was not going to give up now. Aunt Peggy gave her the phone number and asked that she not repeat to Sophia the things she'd said about her. Mom was furious when Alexandra told her what Aunt Peggy said. Hearing it only served to further drive the nail into the box that held a lifetime of unforgivable things with her sister.

Mom couldn't help but notice how Alexandra was speaking about Jacob Krasnoff with such familiarity. So she asked, "How do you know Jacob Krasnoff?"

"Oh, that's right," said Alexandra. "You don't know anything. I didn't know all of it either until I got my adoption file after my mother died when I was just twenty-three," she said. Alexandra continued to explain how she knew the Savannah attorney who handled the adoption proceedings for Sophia, our mother.

Her adopted mother's name was Heather Flowers. Heather moved to Savannah alone when she was eighteen years old. Not long after being in Savannah, she met the already married attorney Jacob Krasnoff. Alexandra received a box full of love letters along with her adoption file after Heathers' passing when Alexandra was twenty-three years old. The letters revealed a lifetime of promises from Jacob to be with Heather exclusively one day. One day never came, but Jacob did gift his lifelong mistress Heather with someone to love for the rest of her life. At the age of fifty she received Sophia's baby girl whom she named Alexandra. There never was a young Christian couple who couldn't have children. Jacob died just five years later.

Heather and Alexandra continued to live in Savannah until Sophia called Jacobs protégé, James Louis Montgomery, in 1979 to ask about the welfare of her baby. James had taken over Krasnoff's office after his passing. Heather was so afraid of losing Alexandra that they packed everything and moved to Knoxville, Tennessee. Alexandra finished high school and college there. That's where she was living when her mother passed away.

All of those years our mom had pictured her child with a loving Christian couple. She felt so deceived by Jacob, but all of the pieces began to fit. Alexandra continued to tell her that her mother Heather never tried to hide the fact that she was adopted. After all, she didn't look like any of that family. Alexandra was 6 feet tall and her adoptive family, aunts, and cousins were all short.

"Alright!' Mom said. "Another Amazon!" It was a term she loved to use to describe the women in our family. Marilyn is 5" 9' and I'm 6"1'.

"Your sisters are going to be thrilled to meet you," Mom said. "They both know about you Alexandra. I always assumed you were a boy! That nurse was holding yellow clothes." Suddenly she realized that was another curve ball thrown by Jacob.

"I'm sorry to keep interrupting. I still can't believe this is happening," Mom said. Healing tears began to flow down her cheeks again. On the other end of the line, she could tell that Alexandra was emotional also. It was a wonderful day for both of them indeed. After a few moments of quiet, Alexandra continued. She told Mom she'd married a man named John, who her mother Heather despised. They both laughed. She told her how she couldn't wait to become a mother, and after she was, she could imagine how hard it must have been for Mom to let go of her.

Alexandra said she asked her adoptive mother Heather what she knew about her birth mother when she was growing up. Heather told her she'd seen her out one evening in Savannah, that she was a very tall, beautiful blonde who could dance really well. That was the image Alexandra said she kept of our mother her entire life.

"I want you to know something, Sophia." she said, "I had a great life. I had everything I ever wanted. I attended *Savannah Country Day* private school. We had housemaids. Heather did a great job. I was very loved, and I just want to thank you for giving me life. I'm just so grateful for this life."

Mom was too emotional to talk. She held the phone and let the tears flow. "I must come there to meet you," Alexandra said. Mom managed to get a "Yes" out, still consumed with emotion. Mom was so relieved and grateful that Alexandra didn't hate her for giving her up for adoption. Mom was amazed that Alexandra didn't know any of the reasons why she had to give her up, yet Alexandra was already forgiving her for it and was thanking her for life. She was just full of so much gratitude, compassion, and love.

Alexandra mentioned the man Marcus, whose name and letters she had from the adoption file that was given to her when her mother passed. "Yes," said Mom. "Go ahead and reach out to him, darling. I am one hundred percent sure he is your father, and I would be honored to pay for the DNA test to prove it to him if he needs that!"

Alexandra was elated. She went from having her husband, his family, and their children as her only family to finding her birth mother, father, and siblings.

They decided to end the phone call and try to get some rest. Alexandra would call back when she had flights scheduled. Neither of them wanted to hang up the phone. The connection re-established after all these years felt tied to that phone line. They both let go of the phone receivers in tears.

Mom called her mother Doris as soon as she got off the phone. "You won't believe who just called me, mama!" she said.

"Who?" Doris said.

"The baby I had to give up ... it's a girl! And she's coming home!!"

"You're going to be all right now aren't you Sophia?" her mother asked.

Next she called me and Marilyn to share the good news. I was in Watertown, New York visiting my best friend Connie. I answered the phone to hear my weeping mother's broken words. "My baby, my baby, she found me Honey Jo! She's coming home!"

I couldn't believe what I was hearing. Chill bumps covered my body from head to toe. I wanted to say something, but no words could come out of my mouth for what seemed like forever! I was remembering the day my mother sat me down and told me the story. It was only after learning about the baby she had to give up that I realized the reason my mother got so depressed every year in March around her birthday. My heart overflowed with tears of the miracle I knew was for our mother. For all of us, but especially our mother. That empty hole would now be filled and so many questions answered. It was a miracle indeed. Marilyn was also elated to hear the news, to meet the woman she always believed to be a boy like our Mom had assumed all of these years. Any time Marilyn dated someone she found out was adopted she did the math to be sure he couldn't be her brother!

Me, Mom, Marilyn, and Mom's best friend Ivy all went to the Savannah airport to meet Alexandra and her husband's flight. With great anticipation, we watched the plane from Dallas touch down on the runway. The airport had been sectioned off after 9/11, with no one allowed past the security checkpoint. The time from landing to unloading seemed to take forever as we all watched anxiously for people to come over the hill toward the front of the airport where we stood. As Alexandra exited the plane, the airline agent took one look at her and said, "I know where you belong!"

"You do?" she asked. She had a curious look on her face.

"Yes, there's a group of tall women who look just like you at the top of that ramp right there," the agent said. She pointed toward the entrance of the airport. She dropped the handle of her pull behind for her husband John to carry and began to run up the hill as fast as she could. We all knew exactly who she was the instant our eyes made contact with hers. Happy tears streamed down our faces and wide-open arms were eager to embrace her. It was like a missing part of all of us was coming home. Strangers could feel the love emanating from us as they stopped and watched our reunion unfold. I loved being the witness as the emptiness my mom had lived with for so many years seemed to disappear the moment Alexandra entered her arms. I felt as though she was complete in a way she hadn't been since 1965.

CHAPTER 12

The Freedom Plunge

Each of our lives have changed dramatically since the day Alexandra came home.

Mom did get the nerve to leave Kenny after twenty years of marriage. She was able to live alone for the first time in her life and has learned to enjoy the solitude that comes with knowing there won't be anyone coming home drunk and acting crazy. As yet, there doesn't seem to be enough of that peaceful feeling for her to bring those manuscripts back out from under the bed. Her health has continued to deteriorate after having four more spinal operations. I believe her pain is a result of the deep resentment she still holds toward all of the people in her life who wronged her.

She's been in bed for more than ten years now. She lives at my home in Springfield, Georgia. There's still a photograph of my father on her bedside table.

What a blessing it was that day in the hot salty bath when I was finally able to forgive. As if by grace I was given the understanding to be able to see my mother in a different light. That understanding allowed the doors of my heart to open with compassion and empathy. She had a rough go of it right from the beginning.

I try to introduce the same ideas of forgiveness to her, suggesting just as an experiment that she might want to try something. She listens to me intently so I keep on.

"Recent studies have shown that people store old hurts and resentments in their physical bodies as pain. I was thinking, just as an experiment, perhaps you could play with that concept a little bit. Maybe you could start with your earliest memories, and each time one of them upsets you, take a moment to forgive the person who you feel wronged you. Maybe you could forgive yourself if you felt you wronged them. Like the prayer Jesus taught his disciples to pray. 'Forgive us our trespasses, as we forgive those who trespass against us.'"

She listened to me but became defensive when I said something about loving your brother as yourself. She was thinking I was going to try to get her to see her brother. He's been over several times knocking on the door. I believe he wants to resolve things before he leaves this earth. He's eighty-five years old now, but she won't let him in. So I decided to be quiet about it. I gave it to God, and I released my own expectations of her being able to do it. Perhaps a seed was planted and she would at least consider what I said.

Friends? She has one, Ivy, who I'm convinced is an angel. She still comes over to visit Mom often, always bringing a little something special to brighten her day.

My sister Marilyn always said that the women in our family were under a curse. Mom even said that a man who frequented a bar where she worked once told her that in another life she'd been a man who treated women horribly. He told her she would pay off this karmic debt in this lifetime by never being happy with a man. While that does sound like a curse, I'm not too sure I believe all of that.

There's something I've come to know as true. We come into this world pure and void of judgment. Empty, like a new computer. As children, we have little say over how things go in our lives. We just ride along with the choices being made for us by our "tribe" or "family." They download the programs. We have their behaviors, beliefs, judgments, fears, expectations, and rituals, consciously or subconsciously. That's exactly how they were raised too.

Here are some of the beliefs I was given. When life gets tough you send your kids away until you get it straightened out. If life gets too hard you leave and go somewhere else. Your worth will be determined by how you look and behave. You won't have the love and respect of a man if you aren't thin and in shape. What other people might think of you will be valued enough to control your life and the decisions you make. If your behavior is upsetting to someone else, change it to accommodate them. Never bitch, nag, or complain. Men don't like that. If you sin, you'll have hell to worry about. Guilt is a productive emotion. If you're not doing something every day you're a lazy person. Don't be a lazy person. And the list just goes on and on. Especially if it was a strong belief in our families, we most likely adopted it. It wasn't all bad. I was given some good ones too. We know the difference. One feels good ... one does not.

At some point during our grown-up lives we have to look into ourselves, into our "computers" or "minds." We need to ask the questions about how much of what's in there is actually serving our highest good. How much of it is serving the betterment of our world?

Here's the simplest question to ask ourselves to get a hint of what may be hiding in there. Does this make me feel good about who I am? If the answer is no, then *don't do it, don't say it,* and when you're in the master class, you'll learn, *don't think about it* either! Yes ,we can and should learn how to master our own thoughts. Let's all at least be willing to delete the mind viruses that keep running the same programs of suffering and unhappiness that we receive and then pass on generation to generation.

It seems far easier to look around and find what's wrong with everyone else in our lives and in our world.

Long and narrow is the road to the journey within seeking what needs to change, but this road leads to freedom! We become empowered to break the chain of generational conditioning. Freeing first ourselves and then our world.

I struck out for the third time in the marriage arena in 2002. I noticed the common denominator in three failed marriages: Me! I took myself to a therapist who told me that because of my upbringing I would always choose the wrong partner. He said you could walk into a room with a hundred men in it, and you would automatically be drawn to the worst one for you. After leaving his office I felt hopeless for a future with any kind of normal relationship.

But rather than accept that as my future I decided to dive into every book, class, or seminar I could get my hands on about looking within, about relationships, and codependency. It was hard to look inside myself and see how I contributed to my own failures, how I sabotaged my own happiness. The information I was absorbing didn't change me overnight, but change did come. I continue to grow and evolve.

I'm excited now about the impact of quantum healing. What is quantum healing you ask? Remember the story of my classmate who went home to clean her whole house after I massaged her? Remember I was only thinking about cleaning the whole time I worked on her? I never verbalized any of my thoughts yet she went home and cleaned her whole house. This is how science is now proving thoughts produce form. If we

Great to have all this time to focus on yourself

are mindful of our thoughts, and if we can change what we believe, we can change everything. I believe this is the future of our healing capabilities. Oh so simple but that's how the Divine works. I also like to imagine what life would be like for all of us without expectations. We can only be hurt, disappointed, angry, and full of resentment if WE have an expectation that is unmet by someone else. We really give our power away when we expect anything to be other than what it is. If we're going to expect anything let it be that we will suffer and experience pain as long as we have expectations.

The next time I put a wedding gown on was in 2012, on a girlfriend weekend down at Tybee Island when two of my best girlfriends woke up with me before dawn to go down to the ocean where I made some vows to myself. I vowed to be true to me. To only do what made me feel good about who I am. I forgave myself and others for my painful past and plunged in!

For each of us, it's never too late to choose again. To choose love, to forgive, or to change a long-held, deep-seated belief that is no longer serving us. Make some vows to yourself and jump into that great big ocean of life! Emerge FREE and enjoy the journey down your own Salt Creek Road.

What has happened in my life since I made those vows and took the plunge is simply incredible. But that's another story ... until then

"Have salt in yourselves, and be at peace with one another" (Mark 9:50 ESV)

In LOVE,
Honey Jo

PS: I would love to see your "freedom plunges!" Please share them with me on Instagram.

Honey Jo with friends Latrelle and Jill

Sisters

CPSIA information can be obtained
at www.ICGtesting.com
Printed in the USA
LVHW040928251120
672637LV00006B/181